40 Days to Balanced Parenting

‰

How to Bring Your Busy Life Back into Balance

‰

By Erin Brown Conroy, MA, MFA

Celtic Cross Communications

First edition. Third printing
ISBN 0-9740981-1-6
Self help/relationships/family/health/parenting

Dedication

To my Children –
Each one a gift from God,
Precious and valued more than they'll ever know,
Who have taught me that no matter what happens in life,
No matter where we come from or where we've been,
No matter what has happened in the past,
This very moment
and the way we love and respond to each other right now
is what matters the most.

"Have I told you yet today what a treasure you are to me?"

Contents

ತಿ⊷

40 Days to Balanced Parenting

How to Bring Your Busy Life
Back into Balance

❧

Introduction

What This Workbook will Do for You

❧

Parenting is one of the most rewarding, joyous experiences on this earth. And it's one of the most challenging. Whether your child is newborn or in high school, trying to "fit it all in" with our families is hard to do. Life seems to tip out of balance so very quickly. Balance – that sense of **steadiness and stability in a schedule that feels good and keeps us healthy** – is something that we long for with a passion. And it can be oh, so elusive.

We're busy. Our lives are full. In fact, parenting is downright demanding. Trying to balance demands drains our personal resources. We're stressed. We're worn down and tired. We may even get physically sick from putting out so much energy. And then we end up sick and tired of being sick and tired.

Balance doesn't just "happen." Balance is something that's purposefully created, something that's gained. Like a teeter-totter, the ability to balance our lives swings in and out, through seasons and experiences – planned and unplanned. Life has a way of knocking us off balance – often. We find ourselves swinging out of balance when we least expect it. The "trick" as a busy parent is to shift our lives, in order to be able to come back to center. How do we live in "balanced parenting"? The answer lies within the process of continuing to find the place of balance.

Time management is a multi-million dollar industry. Finding balance is a hot topic. Each year, publishers blitz us with thousands of books on time management – and balancing our lives.

So what makes *40 Days to Balanced Parenting* so special? It's specifically designed for you, as a parent. Parenting has a unique dynamic attached to day-to-day living. The principles and methods of Balanced Parenting work within those unique dynamics. I know. As a parent of 13 children, someone asks almost every day, "How do you do it?" This is how. Would you like balance in your life? Do this. Completely. Thoroughly. With thought and focus. The payoff is incredible.

Preface

Exactly What Will I Get Out of this Workbook?

୬ఌ

Everything. Or nothing.
You'll get out of it exactly what you put into it.

Oh, how we hate to hear that, don't we? Come on! That means I'll have to put out *time* and *energy* – and that's exactly what I *don't have enough of!*

Precisely.

That's why you absolutely NEED to step back and take this time – so that you get to the point where you HAVE the time. It's an oxymoron – a riddle – a catch 22, isn't it? The truth remains: **Until we stop and take the time to re-do what's "going wrong" right now, we'll never get to the "right."**

So how badly do you want to be balanced? How strongly do you want to enjoy life? How much do you want to be healthy in your body, mind, soul? How much would you like to be truly happy and enjoying life, no matter the outside circumstances? If you want it, you'll get it. Your strong desire and focus will absolutely get you there, through this 40-day program.

Where does this program come from? What's it based on? And how do I know it will work for me?

Balanced Parenting **comes from research and reality.** It's based on:

*   Over 30 years of examining thousands of reliable books and articles on healthy balanceOver 30 years of examining research-based studies on wellness
*   Over 12 years experience teaching time management, prioritization, and finding balance to university students
*   Over 30 years working individually with parents and children one-on-one and in groups
*   25 years discussing real-life struggles with moms and dads in "real life" – over cups of coffee, standing at sports activities, and waiting in hallways during music lessons
*   24 years counseling families
*   47 years of invaluable missteps, oversights, blunders, tragedies, heartbreaks, problems, struggles, difficult dilemmas, poor choices, bad decisions, wrong turns, and terrible mistakes – that sifted out truth, understanding, insight, hope, optimism, strength, joy, enjoyment, and understanding the value of every breath – to the top of it all

This program will work for you because it's based on true principles and tested in real life.

The *Balanced Parenting* program does three things:

- FIRST – It helps you to identify what's important, bringing you to the bottom-line question: What is my life's deep-down, inner purpose? How does that purpose relate to my family and children? Knowing what drives us and motivates us daily – and being able to center on what's really important – is the foundation to putting our time all together as a parent.

- SECOND – It helps you shed light on your current use of time, answering the questions, "How am I spending my time right now? When I hold my current use of time up to the light of what's really important to me – my purpose – does it match?"

- THIRD – It gives you a framework of accountability for change. It's a guide and outline that, if followed, reminds you daily of what you can – and must – do to create and follow through with changes that bring balance to you life. If we consistently make changes over 40 specific days, those changes are more likely to become a part of who we are. We grow new habits, both in thinking and acting. We bring our purpose into alignment with our everyday use of time, creating a much more balanced life.

Balancing in tandem

Last summer, our family spent a day on Mackinac Island near the Upper Peninsula in Michigan. Mackinac Island is a beautiful place, from the rocky white shoreline to the quaint shops, gorgeous homes, and historical fort. One of the special things about Mackinac is that no cars or motor vehicles are allowed on the island. To travel about, you walk, ride a horse, or ride a bike. We decided it would be a great experience to take the whole family around the island on bikes. Two mountain bikes pulling carts behind with two preschoolers in each, two child-sized bikes, and three tandem bikes later, we were off.

Our six teenagers and middle-schoolers rode the three tandem bikes. My husband and I exchanged a few broad smiles watching them learn how to balance and work together. The importance of the lead person – the "driver" – became immediately clear. Once in a while, the driver lapsed into thinking only of him or herself and began to steer and move without regard for the person behind. The wild reaction of the rider behind instantly jolted the driver back to "keeping it together" on the front of the bike. By the end of the afternoon, a true team formed on those bikes, and the driver and rider enjoyed the time with each other – and even found themselves talking about their "team" on the bike.

❧

Maintaining a healthy relationship with our child is like riding the tandem bike. As the parent, there are crucial keys to a smooth ride: our driving skills, the direction we take or "drive" our kids, and our attentiveness – our alertness and sensitivity – to how the driver and rider respond and interact.

❧

The driver holds the key responsibility. We hold the responsibility for our personal direction and efforts. Our efforts are directly connected to and influence our child. There's no doubt about it: Healthy parents grow healthy children. **In order to parent our child well, we absolutely must begin with ourselves.** If we maintain our spiritual, mental, emotional, physical, and social health, then we're able to give, respond, and teach our children within a healthy framework that allows us to parent our child with success.

Driving in tandem, we lead and "pull along" our children's health and personal direction. Based on our innermost beliefs, desires, and goals, there are also actions we can – and must – perform or "do" **each day** to maintain healthy relationship with our children. *Balanced Parenting* gives a framework for identifying what's important and tracking daily progress in doing what's right.

This program isn't fluff. It takes commitment. It takes specific time. It takes deep and honest

---

▶ What's this About?
This section tells you the bottom line - the key information to understand.

✓ To Do
This is your "action step". Take time to follow what's suggested, step by step, for the best results.

? Answer these Questions
Think through and describe your answers as completely as possible. Try to avoid one-line answers. do what it takes to think deeply and completely.

✦ My Center
Here's what you want to come away with _ the most important point to remember.

---

thought about what matters most to you. It takes a decision to follow what's really important.

Yes, it involves discipline. It takes faithful dedication to keeping track of a number of areas in your life, for the purpose of accountability. And it takes a commitment of at least 40 days. Sound hard? That depends on you. If you're sick and tired of feeling out of balance, tired of living from stress to stress, and yearning in your heart to really be the best parent that you can be, then you're ready to do what it takes and succeed at this thing called "balance." You can do it.

There are five steps to *40 Days to Balanced Parenting*

1. **Centering on What I Live For.** Days One and Two of the 40 Days, you'll go through a three-page exercise to identify what's most important in your life - your purpose and core values.

2. **Knowing My Foundational Truths.** Days Three and Four are reading days. Your suc-

cess with Balanced Parenting depends on your understanding of foundational truths. Reading and understanding those foundations that give you the basics necessary for your success.

3. **Finding Out Where I Am.** Days Five through Eleven (seven days), you'll keep track of a week of your personal and parenting time and then interpret what you found out. It involves carrying around a one-page chart to fill in as you briefly keep track of where your time and energy is going. We have to know where we are in order to know where we're going and how to get there.

4. **Shifting My Time.** Day Twelve, you'll create an incremental plan to shift the way you spend your time so that it's in line with your purpose and core values. Here's the fun part: dreaming and planning.

5. **Journaling and Creating New Directions.** Days Thirteen through Forty (four weeks), you'll journal your time and efforts, daily reminding yourself of your purpose and holding yourself accountable to seeking and finding balance. At the end of each week, you'll evaluate and adjust, making real and immediate changes that bring balance to your life. Now you're in the thick of it – making real change. Part Five takes the most focus and reaps the most rewards.

And you WILL reap rewards. "Balance" holds all you've ever wanted – personally, professionally, and (most importantly) with your family.

And they're absolutely worth it.

Your visual key

The following signs will help to guide you through *40 Days to Balanced Parenting*. Let's begin by looking at, listening to, and getting a handle on what you live for.

Part One
What's Important to Me?

Days One and Two

Dates: _____

What's Important to Me?
ༀ

As human beings, we're trying – sometimes with disastrous results – to run our businesses, raise our children, teach our students, be involved in our relationships without giving serious and careful consideration to the roots out of which the fruits of our lives are growing.

~Stephen Covey, A. Roger Merrill & Rebecca Merrill,
First Things First (New York: Free Press, 1994, page 30)

What do you live for? What are the utmost reasons for living? What is your purpose in life?

As the quote above states, most of us fail to take the time to consider the "roots of our lives" – our reasons for living. We drive along the lane of life looking at street signs to get our bearings when we don't even know **where we came from or where we're headed.**

▶ What's this About?

If we desire balance, then **our unique and individual purpose – a reason for living and doing what we do – must drive all that we do.** We must choose to spend our time in a way that lines up with what's important. Only then will we measure our time in ways that satisfy us. Only then will we divide our time into meaningful action – in a way that truly balances what we do.

The absolute first step in the process of balancing our lives is figuring out what's important to us.

✓ To Do

Find a quiet place, without interruption and distraction, where you can contemplate and carefully consider the following questions. At least an hour is needed; two or three is best. Fill in your answers with purposeful thought. If you can't think of an answer, then honestly place a question mark in the blank space and spend more time thinking about it. You may want to give yourself a day to contemplate the questions, and then come back with your answers. Either way, your goal is to get something meaningful written in the blanks below within 48 hours.

Don't skip this step! Take the necessary time to lay a strong foundation for the positive change that will happen in the next 40 days.

? Answer these Questions

1. If I knew I had 24 hours to live, and I took a moment to reflect on the whole of my life, what three things would I look back on and feel extremely satisfied about?

_____

_____

_____

_____

_____

_____

_____

_____

_____

_____

2. Is there anything I wish I would have done or been?

_____

_____

_____

_____

_____

_____

_____

_____

_____

_____

_____

3. If I could start my life over, what would I change? What would I do differently?

_____

_____

_____

_____

_____

4. If I could accomplish just one thing in my life, what would that be?

_____

_____

_____

_____

_____

5. What one thing do I want my children to remember me for?

_____

_____

_____

_____

_____

_____

6. Why was I put on this earth?

_____

_____

_____

_____

_____

_____

Look at your answers in the previous questions. Is there a common theme? Is there one thing that jumps out at you? If you wrote, "I don't know," take time to ponder the questions and come back to answer them again. Your goal is to getting answers to what's most important to you and what drives you at the core of your being.

✦ My Center

I was put on this earth to:

_____

_____

_____

_____

I believe my purpose in life is:

_____

_____

_____

_____

The things that are most important to me in my life are:

_____

_____

_____

_____

_____

Part Two

Foundational Truths

Days Three and Four

Dates: _____

Foundational Truths

ক্ষ

Know and understand the blueprint,
and you'll know and understand what to do;
follow the blueprint, and you'll get what you want.
EBC

▶ What's this About?

There are five areas to balance in our lives: Spiritual, Mental, Emotional, Physical, and Relational. Most of your work in bringing your life back into balance through *40 Days to Balanced Parenting* involves journaling what's going on in your life in these five areas. This is a brief overview of each area of foundational truth that leads to balance.

✓ To Do

Take time to read through and contemplate each of these areas and how they relate to your life.

1. Spiritual Wellness

ক্ষ

You will know the truth, and the truth will set you free.
John 8:32, the Bible

We are spiritual beings, with a spirit – a soul. There's an inner part that loves, strives, and yearns for connection with others and with God. Have you ever been "moved" by a piece of music? Have you been "touched" by a photo of a hurting child and felt a welling-up of inner conviction to help the child, in a strength that originates beyond yourself? Have you stood in beautiful surroundings and felt an inner peace that transcends description? Each of us has placed within us a place for experiencing deep spirit and soul connections such as these.

We each also have a piece deep within which hungers for connection with our Creator. We can ignore that piece, eventually becoming numb to it, or we can nurture that piece, becoming more whole human beings, eventually connecting with God in a way that we would never have imagined possible.

"How much do I pay attention to the spiritual side of my life?" *Balanced Parenting* not only acknowledges our spiritual side, but it also presents Spiritual Wellness as the first and foremost part of finding balance in our lives. All of who we are stems from the root of spiritual connection. Ignoring our Spiritual Wellness is like trying build the framework for your home on swampland.

Spiritual Wellness begins with contemplating and connecting with God. It means reaching out from with ourselves from a point of honest reflection and humility to truly seek God and His Truth. The Bible states that if truly seek God with all our hearts, we'll find Him. Seeking Truth will only do one thing for me: It will give me a firm basis for all of my life experience, providing a solid fulcrum for true balance.

"What do I believe?" What efforts have I made to connect with God? How important is a relationship with God to me? Why is it important? Why not? If I currently value building a relationship with God and connecting to Him, does that show up in the way I spend my time? Does it resound in what I do with my child? Does it rise up into all areas of my life? Why or why not? If we want to feel balance each day, we can't ignore these questions. Because how I respond to life is rooted in what I believe.

Connecting with God takes effort. He reaches to us, but our responsibility is to respond back to Him. We can connect with God in three ways:
- Speaking to Him out loud or within our minds (prayer),
- Listening to what He has to say through taking in information (reading or listening), and
- Taking positive actions of love toward others (doing).

In *Balanced Parenting,* **you'll be asked to journal these things:**

Contemplating God

What are my thoughts about Who God is? God shows Himself in many ways. He's powerful. He provides. He takes care of me. He gives me good things, including my children. What attributes, or characteristics, of God are meaningful to me?

God, I need to make things right with you with...

We all fail. We all make mistakes. Admitting failure doesn't make us weak. It does the exact opposite; it takes a strong person to admit failure. When we admit our failure, we move forward and grow beyond the failure. If we deny our faults, we become not only blind to them, but we also become prideful and arrogant. Honest reflection allows us to make adjustments in our personal wellness. Ultimately, we need to answer the question, "What parts of my life do I feel or believe need to shift, in order to align with God's good and perfect Will for me?"

Thank you, God, for...

Being mindful of the good things that we have creates an attractive attitude of gratefulness. Daily listing the relationships, things, and activities that we're feeling grateful for creates an attitude that transforms us into something appealing on the inside. Realizing the awesome opportunity we're given to love and live each day gives us mental and emotional attractiveness to others.

God, I need your guidance and help for...

Leaning on the Creator of the universe isn't a crutch – it's smart! If I had trouble with my computer, I'd seek out and rely on the knowledge and direction of a technical specialist – and I'd reap the benefits of leaning on his guidance. The same goes for God; leaning on His guidance is an intelligent thing to do.

I ask wisdom for...

Wisdom is at the core of good decisions, for ourselves and for our children. What's coming up in my day that's important to me? What knowledge do I need for making good decisions on this particular day?

Reading

We need to put good things into us, every day, in the spiritual sense. If we read good, right, helpful, wise information each day, that information is now accessible and available to us, to become better people and better parents. Keeping track of what we've read helps us to remember what we're read and gives us a resource to refer to in the future.

Thought for Today

Summaries pull the best of the best into one phrase, one sentence. Summarize your thoughts and ideas into something you can hold onto and remember throughout the day.

2. Mental and Emotional Wellness

෬ඏ

As a person thinks, so he or she is
John 8:32, the Bible

Our mind is extremely powerful. What we think and say in our minds guides our emotions and actions. If we think in healthy ways, we then can feel and act in healthy ways.

When I teach leadership courses to university students and adults, those who gain the most visible personal growth and achievement of balance are those persons who truly grasp and understand – and practice – mental and emotional wellness. As you think in your mind, so you are.

If there's nothing else that you take to heart in this section, understand this truth:

> *What I believe in my heart to be true leads me to my thoughts. What I think leads me directly to how I feel. How I feel drives me to how I act.*

Here's an example of how this truth works:

If I **believe** that my child doesn't care about me or anyone else, then I **think** that his rude behavior comes from his nasty inner spirit. My **thoughts** are, "What a rude child! He doesn't care what's right and wrong. He's just looking out for himself. He's irresponsible and spiteful." These negative **thoughts** lead me to **feelings or emotions** of anger, frustration, and dislike. My **actions**, then, will be negative and angry, not loving and kind.

But if I **believe** that my child is immature, still growing in his ability to **think** and act with good choices that consider others' interests before his own, then I think that his rude behavior comes from lack of maturity and ability. My **thoughts** are, "I need to help my child. He needs to learn right from wrong. He's in a place where he needs guidance. I'm going to help him to become the great person that he can be." These positive **thoughts** lead me to **feelings or emotions** of patience, love, and compassion. My actions, then, will be loving and kind, not negative and angry.

> *We absolutely must put positives thoughts into our minds, for what we put into our minds ultimately shapes all that we are.*

In *Balanced Parenting*, you'll be asked to journal these things:

Positive Input: Reading
> Each day, we must read something that builds our mind in a positive way. Grow your capacity to discover, think, and reason. What great idea did you read that you want to remember?

Positive Input: Beauty
> Our world is full of beauty, from grand sunsets to minuscule perfection of the intricate pattern within the veins of a supple leaf. Soaking in the beauty of creation around us does something incredibly positive to our mind and emotions. There's something

that happens on a higher plane that touches our minds and hearts when we center on something beautiful. Focusing on a moment of beauty grows us emotionally.

3. Physical Wellness

୬ৡ

Maximum bodily strength and efficiency depend upon three factors:
sleep, exercise, and nutrition.

Dr Martin Shaffer, *Life After Stress*
(New York: Plenum Press, 1982, page 92)

Most programs for personal improvement center only on physical wellness. Remember, you are a complex being; every part of your being relates together for balance. We can't totally center on the physical part of balance, and we can't ignore the physical part either. We have to consider physical wellness equally with all the rest.

> *Balanced Parenting isn't designed to make you a model or a bodybuilder – although it could! Balanced Parenting helps you to feel better physically and become balanced in all areas of your life. Your physical state affects your mind, emotions, spiritual focus, and relationships with others. There's a huge connection between physical wellness and your entire life's balance.*

In *Balanced Parenting,* you'll be asked to journal these things:

Exercise

Balanced physical exercise is divided into three areas:
- Aerobic/Cardiorespiratory Endurance,
- Strength, and
- Flexibility.

In order to be balanced, you must be aware of and take into consideration all three.

Aerobic/Cardiorespiratory Endurance is that "at least three times a week, get your heart rate up" recommendation from the experts that you always hear about. Running, walking, cycling, spinning, aerobics videos, swimming, and anything else that gets the blood pumping for 20 minutes or more qualifies.

Strength training is weight training. It targets muscles, through resistance of some kind, including free weights or machines.

Flexibility is stretching, bending, and fighting tightness or stiffness. Yoga or daily relaxation stretches create flexibility. If we want to be at our personal level of optimum health, we must have some of each of these areas of exercise in our lives.

Nutrition

What goes into our mouths? Drinking the right amounts of water, eating the right kinds of foods, and taking vitamins or supplements all fall into the area of "balanced nutrition." Here's an area where a lot of people struggle for balance. This program gives practical ideas for nutritious eating for busy parents – And these are ideas that *work*.

4. Social/Relational Wellness

✳

Love is not like other resources....
The more it is used, the more its supply increases.

Dr. Richard Swenson, *Margin*
(Colorado Springs: Navpress, 1992, page 240)

"No man is an island." We are social beings. In order to be balanced, we need positive, balanced relationships.

When we become parents, our social life often suffers. When they're babies, we focus our waking moments on the helpless, red-faced bundle that eats, sleeps, messes diapers, and then starts the whole cycle over again.

When our kids are toddlers, we spend our time following them around so they don't break something, fall off something, swallow something, or kill something.

When they're preschoolers, we spend our waking moments answering questions, playing dolls and cars, reading books, and bandaging scrapes.

When they're in school, we help them learn and deal with emotional tragedies such as "Jared doesn't like me anymore."

When they're in middle school, we deal with misbehavior (of others and sometimes our own kids), friendships gained and lost, and driving to sports and music events.

When they're teens, we spend our time checking in, listening, driving, and then worrying when they're driving themselves.

Who in the world has time for a social life?! And if you have two, four, or more kids, what is a social life?!

> *Loving our children is a wonderful thing. But loving our children often depletes us. We can't just give and give, or there will be nothing left. We must also receive levels of love, from both our children and other adults. In order to be a healthy and balanced person, we must nurture relationships and interaction with others on a social level.*

The way we manage our time needs to include social, relational interaction.

In *Balanced Parenting*, you'll be asked to journal these things:

Positive Input: People
> We need to spend quality time with others that builds us up internally, as people. Who we spend time with greatly influences our attitudes and thoughts. Negative people

tear us down; positive people grow us. Negative perspectives and complaining tears us down; mentally stimulating conversations that focus on hope, health, and giving to others grows us. We're "filled up" when we have healthy face-to-face interactions with others, as we communicate through words, body language, and listening and understanding.

Positive Input: Phone Calls

Phone calls are legitimate connections with others. When we speak, we're touching each others' lives. When it comes to socially connecting with others, phone calls "count."

Positive Input: The Written Word (emails, letters)

The art of written communication is coming back a bit with the Internet and email/instant messaging. The written word can be poignant, significant, and strong in building relationships with others. Whether it's a simple card in the mail, a long letter, or an instant message "hello," written words connect us.

Each area is important for balancing our lives:
Spiritual, Physical, Mental, Emotional, and Social.

We are intricate persons, and when it comes to "balance," every area of our lives weaves together to create a life that's healthy and strong.

Part Three
Finding Out Where I Am
∾∾

Days Five through Eleven

Dates:_____

What's My Life Like Right Now?

৩০৫

You've heard the phrase, "I can't see the forest for the tress";
that's nothing –
as parents, our noses are, more times than not,
stuck right up against the bark.
EBC

▶ What's this About?

In order to move forward and bring balance into our busy lives, we first need to take good hard look at what "real life" looks like – from our first moments of waking to climbing back into the sheets at night. We need to answer the smoldering questions, "What's going on in my life right now? What are my days really like? If I stepped out of myself and really saw the "play-back" of my day, what would I think about it?"

Most of us have a skewed view of our lives; either we don't see how busy and out of control our life really is, or we think our schedules are awful when they really aren't. You've probably heard the phrase, "perception is reality." Is it?

I venture to say our minds house our realities more than our bodies. That is, what we think about our days greatly affect the way we respond at any given moment. So what do you perceive life to be? And then, stepping outside of yourself, what do you see? Do you really know how you're spending your time?

✓ To Do

You're going to find out exactly where your time is going. Over the next seven days, use the chart on the following page to literally graph out how you're spending your time. Carry the graph with you. Rip the page right out of this workbook and literally stick it inside something important, like your date book or calendar. Yes, that's right: Physically carry it everywhere you go. Why? You want a true-to-life account of your hours, and the only real way to do that is to carry the page with you everywhere.

There isn't a whole lot of space to write; just use "S" for sleep or "W" for work; I'm sure you get the idea. However you mark the page, keep it a true account of your time. When you're done with the week, answer the questions on the page following the chart. Keep a good account; you'll be glad you did.

Turn the page and take a look...

My Personal Time Log

	Monday	Tuesday	Wednesday	Thursday	Friday	Saturday	Sunday
12-1 AM							
1-2 AM							
2-3 AM							
3-4 AM							
4-5 AM							
5-6 AM							
6-7 AM							
7-8 AM							
8-9 AM							
9-10 AM							
10-11 AM							
11-12 PM							
12-1 PM							
1-2 PM							
2-3 PM							
3-4 PM							
4-5 PM							
5-6 PM							
6-7 PM							
7-8 PM							
8-9 PM							
9-10 PM							
10-11 PM							
11-12 PM							
Exercise							
Mental Wellness							
Relational Wellness							
Spiritual Wellness							

✓ To Do - When your week is complete

Looking at How You Spent Your Week
How it Feels

If you're like me, when the schedule's down in black and white, I feel a mixture of feelings as I glance over how I spent my week. Putting all of our week down on paper is good in that we're held accountable for how our minutes and hours ticked by. There it all is, staring us in the face. We've tracked our time, we're literally holding the record in our hands, and we can see what we've been doing with our life. Awareness is the first step in everything, especially in balancing our lives as parents.

Finding the Good

First, find the things on How I Currently Spend My Time that you feel good about. Put a star over or highlight those things you believe are worthwhile and valuable to you and your family. We're going to want to copy these positive things – and even better them.

Finding the Not-So-Good

Next, let's look at those things that surprised and even embarrassed us.
- Especially pay attention to the hour totals at the bottom of the time log.
- Circle the choices that you made that you believe "wasted" your time. Now it's very important that at this point you don't get down on yourself for what you consider poor use of your time. Look at this particular week as a valuable piece of information that's going to allow you to move forward into getting your life balanced.
- Mentally scrutinize your schedule. How? Emotionally separate yourself, as if you were someone else with a notepad, looking into your life through a window and marking down observations from a more clinical perspective.

? Answer these Questions

1. Total the number of hours in the categories listed at the bottom of the page. What do you think of the number of yours you spent in sleep?

    _____

    _____

    _____

    _____

    _____

2. What do you think of your hours spent in purposeful exercise?

    _____

    _____

    _____

    _____

    _____

3. How much time did you spend each day that qualifies as "growing your mind," putting positive new ideas and thoughts into your mind through reading, listening, or watching something of value?

    _____

    _____

    _____

    _____

    _____

4. How much time each day did you positively relate to others, with stimulating, meaningful, deep conversation? How much time was spent building relationships with others?

    _____

    _____

    _____

    _____

    _____

5. How much time did you spend each day growing the spiritual part of who you are? How much time praying? Reading? Thinking? Listening?

    _____

    _____

    _____

    _____

    _____

Look at your answers above. Is there a common theme? Is there one thing that jumps out at you? Your goal is to get a true snapshot of "a week in the life of me." What do you think of what you see?

Change

My guess is that you see some things that you'd like to change. In fact, if you do this exercise every week for the next year, I'll bet that 99.9% of the time, you'll find something that you want to change. Life has a funny habit of flying by in a way that we don't expect it to. And, as people, we have a funny (and sometimes not so funny) habit of spending our time in ways that, in retrospect, we'd like to change. Be specific. Identify your change areas.

✦ My Center

When I look at how I spent my time this week, I feel good about:

_____
_____
_____
_____
_____

When I look at how I spent my time this week, I don't feel good about:

_____
_____
_____
_____
_____

What surprised me the most was:

_____
_____
_____
_____
_____

The "bottom line" from this exercise - what I discovered the most - is:

_____
_____
_____

The Next Step

In the next section, you'll create a plan that is a realistic, measurable change from how you currently use your time.

Part Four
Shifting My Time

Day Twelve

Date:_____

Where Do I Want to Be?

ഗ൶ൢ

To dream and cast a vision for your future is not just to
Walk along the shore of the river
to eventually get to the place where you'll swim;
To dream and cast a vision for the future is to
Step into the river right now, feel its rush and momentum,
and realize...
*You're already in the river - **right now.***
EBC

▶ What's this About?

We've seen what we have in our lives, at this moment. We've looked reality square in the face. "Good" or "bad," it's our reality.

Now's the time to make a plan – now's the fun part. Now is the time to open our minds to what we WANT to be, how we WANT to live our lives. Our dreams ARE our future. Our goals ARE not just tomorrow's reality - they are TODAY'S reality. Our vision IS in existence TODAY.

Let me explain: Once we dream, we are suddenly in the momentum of that dream. We step into our goal, as stepping into a sweeping rush of a river. The rush and pull of the water not only takes us down the river to a new place, it IS the river. You're not waiting to get in the river; you are IN the water, feeling it's wetness, its rush and pull.

When we decide and take just one step – then we are IN the river and experiencing the river. We may not be down stream to the place we're going....But there's absolutely no doubt that we'll be there soon, because we're not on the shore anymore. We're moving.

What is your river? Our dream is a river. Our goal is a river. Do you fully grasp this? Because grasping this truth changes our attitude. Once we step into it, we are IN its existence. We're not on the shore anymore.

There are certain physical constraints on our lives; we can't step into a river that's a mile away from where we stand. But we can step into the river that holds our particular possibilities. More times than not, we hold back from what we really wish and dream for ourselves. What do you dream about...

- With your relationship with your child?
- With your spouse,?
- In how you want to look and feel?

- When it comes to where we want to go?
- When it comes to how you experience life each day.

Usually, there is a better, more relaxed, less stressed, more joyful, more peaceful, more satisfying place to be – And we just haven't stepped into the river yet.

Now you'll step in. It all begins with your dream.

✓ To Do

In the next pages, you'll create an incremental plan to shift the way you spend your time so that it's in line with your purpose and core values. Do you remember what you wrote on those pages in the first section? Do you recall the things you discovered – what meant the most in your life? Go back and look at those pages right now. Those comments are "serious stuff," and we want to take a serious look at what's important to you, so you can get it.

What changes need to be made in the way you spend your time, in order to get to the end results you want in your spirit, body, mind, emotions, and relationships with others? That's what we're going to figure out.

First, let's have a bit of fun. Fill in the next page with what you'd consider the ultimate way to spend your time – with your family, with your job, and the time you spend just on you. This isn't a picture of "reality," by any means; it's meant to be a "way out there – woo-hoo! – ultimate – wild-and-crazy" kind of dream of the way you'd like to spend your time "in a perfect world."

Go ahead....What would your ULTIMATE life be like?

My Ultimate Dream Time Plan

	Monday	Tuesday	Wednesday	Thursday	Friday	Saturday	Sunday
12-1 AM							
1-2 AM							
2-3 AM							
3-4 AM							
4-5 AM							
5-6 AM							
6-7 AM							
7-8 AM							
8-9 AM							
9-10 AM							
10-11 AM							
11-12 PM							
12-1 PM							
1-2 PM							
2-3 PM							
3-4 PM							
4-5 PM							
5-6 PM							
6-7 PM							
7-8 PM							
8-9 PM							
9-10 PM							
10-11 PM							
11-12 PM							
TOTALS							
Sleep							
Exercise							
Mental Wellness							
Relational Wellness							
Spiritual Wellness							

❓ Answer these Questions

1. Even though this was a "wild-and-crazy" exercise, what truths can I pull out of the Ultimate Dream Time Plan just created? Is there anything that jumps out at me as significant, revealing, or surprising?

_____

_____

_____

_____

2. **Looking at how I arranged my schedule,** what underlying values can be seen? Did I put down that I wanted to sleep most of the day? Perhaps I'm feeling my life's too stressed, and the value I want more of is rest in my body, mind, and soul. Did I put in that I'd like to spend four hours a day at the gym? If so, do I really desire a more a healthy, good-looking body, to feel more energy and less stress? Or maybe it's that I want to internally feel good about myself and how I look. Maybe I put a lot of social hours in the day. If so, the value desired is to connect meaningfully with others.

   Do you see how it works? Whatever I place the MOST of in my schedule – that's what I'm really wanting more of in my life. Find out the WHY. Why do you want more time in that activity? Why do you wish you had more of that in your life right now? Try to get down to what's underneath it all, and write your thoughts here:

_____

_____

_____

_____

✓ To Do

Ok, that was fun (at least, I hope it was!). Now let's get serious again. Let's place what we found out into a schedule that shows realistic, meaningful change – change that's played out in "real life" in steps that are doable. Translate the values – what you want more of – into a schedule that you believe you can do . . . with more of what you want . . . reflecting your core values and desires.

The Next Step Time Plan

The goal of your Next Step Time Plan is to move you significantly toward the values expressed in your Ultimate Dream Time Plan.

Fill out your Next Step Time Plan with what you can see happening in the next week, with purposeful awareness of making a change in how you spend your time.

Remember – The goal here is to make a plan that is _balanced_ and _realistic._ When forming your plan, take into consideration:

❑ Sleep – How many hours will you sleep each day, measured in realistic change, for right now?

- Exercise – What amount and type of exercise will you put into your schedule that moves you toward your ultimate goal?

- Mental Wellness – What time will you spend positively growing your mind?

- Relational Wellness – How much time will you spend positively relating to family and friends?

- Spiritual Wellness – How much time will you spend in prayer and putting spiritual information into your life?

> *This is the Time Log that we're going to work toward implementing in the next four weeks.*

These are the changes that we're going to place into our days, hours, and minutes – changes that will move us toward a more BALANCED way of living. This new Next Step Time Plan is drawn out as something in between your Personal Time Log (of your "right now," every day reality) and your Ultimate Dream Time Plan. Go ahead: put it on paper now.

My Next Step Time Plan

	Monday	Tuesday	Wednesday	Thursday	Friday	Saturday	Sunday
12-1 AM							
1-2 AM							
2-3 AM							
3-4 AM							
4-5 AM							
5-6 AM							
6-7 AM							
7-8 AM							
8-9 AM							
9-10 AM							
10-11 AM							
11-12 PM							
12-1 PM							
1-2 PM							
2-3 PM							
3-4 PM							
4-5 PM							
5-6 PM							
6-7 PM							
7-8 PM							
8-9 PM							
9-10 PM							
10-11 PM							
11-12 PM							
TOTALS							
Sleep							
Exercise							
Mental Wellness							
Relational Wellness							
Spiritual Wellness							

Part Five

Journaling and Creating New Directions

∞∾

Days Thirteen though Forty
(Four Weeks)

Recording Progress for Change and Balance
ৡৱ

To do or not to do; that is the question.
EBC

▶ What's this About?

We have a plan. It's time to try it out. For the next four weeks, you're going to keep track of your plan through journaling.

We're talking about your giving out specific, planned, and focused effort again. You might think, "What an incredible amount of time, keeping track of my entire day in a journal – what a pain!" Keeping track DOES take time and effort. But the payoff is ENORMOUS. Do you want the payoff? Keep the journal.

Your journal is your accountability tool. It's the purposeful guide to make purposeful changes. It's the black and white, "in your face" reality of what you're doing – or not doing – to get the results of balanced parenting.

You want the results? Make it happen. You control your hours. You control your days. And if something comes up that throws you off balance, you control how you respond.
- If you're spending time BALANCING your input, creating a healthy mind full of healthy thoughts and attitudes, then physical attacks and spiritual attacks won't get to you.
- If you're taking time to eat, sleep, and exercise well, then your body will feel good and be strong enough to ward off the stress that comes with negativity or poor mental thoughts that others might throw your way.
- If you're taking time to be spiritually grounded, then when your child's illness keeps you up all night, and your body's tired, your spirit and mind will have enough to give what you need to give. It all works together.

You do the work, you get the great results.

✓ To Do

In the next pages, keep track of what you do each and every day. You don't have to write a book; just jot notes. Pencil in key words. Check things off and pen a sentence or two. Use code words, if you like. You're not writing this for anyone but yourself, and you know what you mean. Just try to put something in every section, so you can visibly measure your forward movement towards balance.

What if you get to the end of the week, and things just AREN'T working? Change what you're doing. "Tweak" the plan. Keep "tweaking" until you find out what works. This is your journal, and no one else's – Do what you will to make it work.

Practical Journal How-to's and Secrets for Success

Let's get practical. Here are some "things to do" in order to make the weeks of journaling work.

Motivation

We all need reminders. Some of us get distracted or disinterested more easily than others. Motivational "helps" aren't crutches that show our weakness; they're wise plans for encouragement to keep us on track.

Everyone is motivated by something. You *must* find what motivates you and use it. For some, it can be a threat: "If I don't do this, I'll lose something." For others, it's the carrot on the stick: "If I do this, I'll get something." If you truly identified what's important to you, then the vision of that purpose will pull you forward and compel you to succeed. Only you know what motivates and drives you. Find that vision, grab onto it, and don't let go.

Here are ideas to help build and maintain motivation.

Individual Motivation
- Subscribe to a magazine that fits your desires for physical wellness. Make it a part of your reading for Mental Wellness each day. Keep it in a place that you'll see throughout the day.
- Make a scrapbook or keep a notebook of phrases and stories that encourage
- Make a scrapbook of pictures of those physically fit; cut out pictures from magazines; know what you're aiming for, and keep it in a place where you'll see it and open it often
- Place a verse or phrase of encouragement on a small pieces of paper and stick it in your pocket or place it on your mirror
- If you're at the computer regularly, put a motivating phrase on your screen saver or tape it right on to your computer
- Be your best cheerleader; tell yourself often, within your mind, how you are succeeding that day, at that moment

Motivation with Others
- Meet with an accountability partner regularly
- Call your accountability partner regularly
- If your spouse isn't your accountability partner, let your spouse know what some of what you're doing each day
- Have a weekly meeting with one or more parents going through 40 Days to Balanced Parenting together

Keeping the Journal
The journal is your number one accountability guide. It shows you, in black and white, what's

really going on in your life: where things are working and where they aren't. When I use the program, my journal goes everywhere with me. It's always by my side or in my hands.

Let's be real: Carrying a journal and writing in it is a pain. It's not normal. It's in the way of just living life.

But that's what it's *supposed* to be. You're purposefully interrupting your life that isn't working and making a change. Change is uncomfortable. Expect it to be uncomfortable. Know that the discomfort or oddity that you're feeling is good, because it's the feeling of change, bringing you to the place where you ultimately want to be.

If you've kept a journal before (or if you like to write), the journal shouldn't be too much of an inconvenience...once you're in the habit of filling it out. But if writing's something you tend not to do on a regular basis, then journaling might seem as comfortable as a pack of rocks on your back.

Here are some ideas to help you journal for four weeks.

- o   If you're a morning person, set your alarm 10 to 15 minutes earlier to write in the journal
- o   If you're a night person, do something in your journal in the morning, even if you're a night person; then read/fill it out more completely at night
- o   When writing in the journal, jot down key words and phrases; don't write a book
- o   Put your journal in the same place each day; I put it on the nightstand for a "first thing in the morning" reminder of my goal to be consistent
- o   When I'm home, I carry the journal to the kitchen and keep it on the counter in a conspicuous place for most of the day for two reasons: 1) It's right there to fill out as needed, and 2) It a visual reminder of my commitment to balanced living
- o   Buy an inexpensive plastic holder that holds papers upright (like those used to hold papers upright at your keyboard or desk) and put it on your kitchen counter or table; place your journal on it for easy access
- o   Take your journal to work, and place it in a conspicuous place

Spiritual Wellness

Whether you're used to putting time into your spiritual side or not, Spiritual Wellness is hard to maintain. Like every area of wellness, it doesn't just happen; it takes effort. If this is new to you, stick with it.

Spiritual Wellness brings personal growth beyond what you imagine. If you're one who's valued Spiritual Wellness before, I challenge you to be consistent. Because we all know... Anyone can speak words of intent; not everyone can follow through in a lifestyle that's consistent. With Spiritual Wellness, as in all the areas of wellness, reality lies in doing.

> *Saying that I value Spiritual Wellness is one thing; actually spending consistent time building my Spiritual Wellness is another.*

Prayer

- Set a time each day for "serious prayer" – purposeful connection. It doesn't have to be long, just consistent.
- Pray like talking, at any time, any place, whispering from your heart what's honest and real
- If you've been going through a particularly tough time and find it hard to find things to be thankful for, buy the book 1001 Things to be Thankful For and read it to stir your mind and emotions toward thankfulness
- Most of us know prayer as "telling" – talking toward God, often asking Him to do things for us. But that's not all prayer is. At least half of prayer is "listening" – being quiet in mind and spirit, taking in the calm that comes from the center of listening

Reading

- With your Bible is your foundation and guide, use a version that's clearly understandable. I like the New International Version (NIV) for clarity and the Amplified Bible and Message Bible for giving great descriptive words that I can resonate with
- Keep your Bible out to use, not to gather dust
- When reading the Bible, read only a few verses at a time in order to think clearly about and process through the meaning of what you've read
- Use a daily guide for spiritual growth that's specific and short

Mental and Emotional Wellness

Your mind is powerful. What you do is determined by what you feel; what you feel is determined by what you think and believe. What you say to yourself leads you to what you are at the moment, as well as the person you will become tomorrow.

We absolutely must be aware of what we're saying to ourselves in our heads. Our mental and emotional wellness depends on it. Here are some practical ways to grow mentally and emotionally in a positive way.

Positively Growing My Mind

- Be a person who continues to learn – for life: Seek out quality information that grows you; read snippets of magazine articles to whole books that lift up your mind and attitude
- Keep a magazine in the car, for free moments that spring up unexpectedly
- Highlight, cut out, and save profound pieces of information in a file, envelope, box, or drawer that you can revisit
- Put a CD or cassette player in the bathroom and play positive music at the start of the day
- Put a CD or cassette player in the room of the house that you spend most of your time in, and play positive music or healthy thinking programs
- Buy video series for personal growth and watch a little bit each day; or one day a week, set an appointment to watch the video
- Be aware of the "worldview" presented in the music and videos that you play within your home; choose uplifting, encouraging themes that support a healthy mental view of living
- Take advantage of informational and personal growth workshops and classes at church, community centers, and hospitals

o Go to a personal growth seminar at least once a year

Attitude

The most attractive part of you is your attitude. The most telling part of who you are on the inside is your attitude. What people remember about you is your attitude. Your attitude is the core of your being, from which springs the "ambience" of what others feel when they're around you.

o Be aware of your inner words; take a few seconds to respond by listening to your inner words; stop yourself and reword negative inner words to positive

o Watch your spoken words; take a split-second before you speak to check what you're going to say before you say it, and only say things that you'd want to hear from others to you

o Attitude doesn't just "happen" – it's sown, tended, and reaped; concentrate on sowing seeds of good attitude each and every morning, before you even step out of bed

Beauty

As much as you can be in control of your "beauty input." In your home, surround yourself with beauty. Outside of your home, choose to be aware of the beautiful instead of what's wrong. Beauty permeates life, even in the darkest places; it's up to us to be aware of that beauty and let it influence who we are.

o Create beauty in your home: Choose colors in your home that please you; put a bit of nature in your home such as an arrangement of spring leaves, summer flowers, or fall pine cones; make a place that's comfortable to sit with pillows or a chenille throw; light candles and turn down lights; open windows; play music in the background; have at least one area in your home that you keep picked up and straightened

o Women, take time to feel beautiful: Be "up on" fashion and attractive clothing; dress well; take care of yourself with hot showers and baths that feel great; use fragrance in shower soaps, hand soaps, and sprays; throw away the holey sweats for bed and put on classy sleepwear

o Men, take care of yourself: Wear classy clothing that's up-to-date; keep groomed and clean shaven, even if you don't feel like it; keep your hair trimmed and combed, presenting yourself well at home and in public

o Take time to give yourself at least one "detail" each day – polish your shoes with a throw-away polishing wipe stashed in the glove compartment of the car, wear a piece of jewelry, or take the extra two minutes to make yourself feel "just right" in the way that you're "put together"

o Get in the habit of looking for beauty in the "everyday": a design in nature; a sleek line of landscaping, a building, or a car; the color of someone's eyes; the design on a countertop at the coffee shop; the dance between lighting and shadows in a room

o Enjoy the taste of foods: Don't just eat to replace fuel; take time to breathe deeply and taste fully; avoid eating in the car; make it a point to sit down and purposefully enjoy a meal

Physical Wellness

Our physical state influences our mental, emotional, social-relational, and even spiritual states. There are hundreds of programs for physical wellness. Here are some ideas that work for busy parents.

Sleep

- Give the kids a bedtime and give yourself a bedtime. Stick with it. Go to bed early.
- If you're home with a little one who naps, resist the temptation to do a project during the naptime; instead, rest yourself
- Sleep with pleasure: Wear comfortable sleepwear; use a quality pillow and comfortable sheets and comforter; run a fan or calming sound for "white noise" that screens out outside sounds; use a baby monitor for your most wakeful child's room, on low volume, so you don't worry about hearing a child; secure your home each night with a routine that settles your mind; use the "tried and true" methods of nighttime calming, including chamomile tea or warm milk and a warm bath or shower
- Wake up with pleasure: Use music instead of a blaring alarm; take a moment to stretch before you jump out of bed; have tea water ready to heat in the microwave or coffee ready to turn on in the coffeemaker

Aerobic Exercise

Keep trying different aerobic exercises and programs until you find one that works for you. Here are some ideas for busy parents:

- Videos, videos, videos: In the comfort of your home, you can choose from hundreds, find a favorite or vary your daily partner from celebrities to fitness gurus; make an appointment on your calendar and stick to it; get up before the kids to do the video, or let the kids watch; they can even do the video with you
- Walk, walk, walk: My best aerobic exercise is when I put my youngest in a backpack on my back and a kid or two in a stroller and just walk; bring a juice box, baggie of cheerios, and a cassette player (for you or the one in the stroller) and just go; take advantage of walk in the mall programs that are held before the mall opens, pushing the stroller alone or with a friend
- Join a gym and set a date for spinning, kickboxing, or whatever aerobic class suits you

Strength Training

Strength training has been touted as the fountain of youth. Why do people avoid it? It's hard work. But the results are invaluable. If you want health that lasts, you must incorporate some kind of Strength Training into your week.

- Know the basics: The principles of strength training are straightforward and sensible; you don't have to become an expert - just learn from the experts; read a fitness magazine or book; visit fitness websites; ask someone who lifts weights for advice; go to a gym and ask for advice; hire a personal trainer for an hour of learning
- Buy a set of simple free weights; set a time on your calendar to use them each day; use them before the kids wake up, give the kids a "quiet time" reading books while you use them, or let your kids "work out" next to you
- If you can't buy weights, use soup cans or household objects

- o Subscribe to a fitness magazine that regularly shows you the principles of Strength Training
- o Who doesn't love a fit middle?! Learn and use abdominal exercises daily; it takes no more than five or ten minutes; your abs are the center of your strength, so keep them fit; do abs first thing in the morning or last thing at night, as a routine; let your kids sit on your feet when you do abs; put your baby on your middle when you do abs – they'll love the ride

Flexibility

While some of us bend like a pretzel, some of us have never been flexible. That's OK, because flexibility can be gained, little by little.

- o Learn stretches from fitness pros' videos, or learn from someone at a gym or fitness center
- o When you wake up in the morning, take a moment to stretch
- o Before you go to bed, have a routine of stretching
- o If you sit at a computer or desk, stretch regularly
- o Try Yoga

Nutrition: Water

Water is the foundation for health. Hydration keeps our body working well, flushes out the nasty stuff from our system, and keeps our brains functioning at their optimum.

- o Place a water bottle on your nightstand; drink before sleeping and if you wake in the night
- o Drink one cup of warm water with lemon first thing in the morning to hydrate and wake your body
- o Buy bottled water; place six to eight bottles on the kitchen counter, in the car, and where you work; drink them throughout the day, to make sure you're getting the amount of water that you need; at the end of the day, fill the bottles from the tap and line them up again for the next day.

Nutrition: Food

What we put into our bodies makes us or breaks us; it's that simple – and that significant. You absolutely must have a plan, or you'll eat anything in sight.

- o Take nutritional supplements. We don't eat 100% right, 100% of the time. Nutritional supplements fill in the gaps and give us what we need to live at our peak performance. Join the program at Totally Fit Mom and receive a free download on "How to Choose the Absolute Best Nutritional Supplements for Maximum Health and Energy."
- o Use a tried-and-true nutritional eating plan. Stick with it.

Social/Relational Wellness

We are relational people. The need for relational connection is built into the fabric of who we are as people. Even if you consider yourself a "loner," there's a part of you that will only be complete if you connect relationally with others. If you want to be balanced, some form of time spent on nurturing relationships is absolutely necessary.

Growing Positive Relationships

Jot a note, make a list on the frig, or keep names on the edge of your daily planner of people you want to connect with. Just seeing their names will make the likelihood of you connecting with them more likely.

- o We know that time with our spouse is necessary for growth. Like the shoe company says, "Just do it." Do it first – 15 minutes together in the morning over a cup of coffee, reading a devotional together, praying together – whatever connects you the most deeply, start out the day with that connection. Life together is so much easier when we connect first.

- o As a single parent, find one or two adults to regularly meet with, and make the time together happen.

- o Make it a point to plan at the beginning of each month at least one family social gathering, one lunch date with another couple, or one evening at the movies with a friend. Put it in the calendar "way out ahead." If for some reason you have to cancel, immediately reschedule another event.

- o Call your mom or dad. They'll love it, and it's good for the both of you.

- o Write a letter to someone who has been a positive influence in your life. It will bless them immensely and stir up gratefulness in your heart.

Now let's get to it.

Balanced Parenting
✍ My Compass
Day 1

Date: _____

I. My Spiritual Wellness
You will know the truth, and the truth will set you free.
John 8:32, the Bible

Prayer

Contemplating God _____

_____

God, I need to make things right with you with _____

_____

Thank you, God, for _____

_____

God, I need your guidance and help for _____

_____

I ask for wisdom for _____

_____

Reading/Thought for Today

_____

_____

II. My Mental and Emotional Wellness
As a person thinks, so he or she is.
John 8:32, the Bible

Positively Growing My Mind

Reading/audio/video _____

Remember this thought today _____

_____

Beauty appreciated _____

III. My Physical Wellness

Maximum bodily strength and efficiency depend upon three factors:
sleep, exercise, and nutrition.
Dr Martin Shaffer, Life after Stress (New York: Plenum Press, 1982, page 92)

Sleep

Hours:		Quality:					
			Poor	Fair	Moderate	Good	Excellent

Uninterrupted? yes/no _____

Exercise

Aerobic _____

Strength _____

Flexibility _____

Nutrition

Water _____ _____ _____ _____ _____ _____ _____
(check mark per 8 oz.)

Food

Breakfast _____

Snack _____

Lunch _____

Snack _____

Dinner _____

Snack _____

Vitamins/supplements _____

_____

IV. My Social/Relational Wellness

Love is not like other resources.... The more it is used, the more its supply increases.
Dr. Richard Swenson, Margin (Colorado Springs: Navpress, 1992, page 240)

Growing Positive Relationships

Face-to-face with others _____

_____

_____

Phone calls/ written words (email/letters) _____

_____

_____

_____

_____

Purposeful, positive actions I give to others today: _____

_____

_____

_____

_____

_____

_____

What I liked about today/What I didn't like and want to change: _____

_____

_____

_____

_____

_____

Balanced Parenting
✍ My Compass
Day 2

Date:_____

I. My Spiritual Wellness
You will know the truth, and the truth will set you free.
John 8:32, the Bible

Prayer

Contemplating God _____

_____

God, I need to make things right with you with _____

_____

Thank you, God, for _____

_____

God, I need your guidance and help for _____

_____

I ask for wisdom for _____

_____

Reading/Thought for Today

_____

_____

II. My Mental and Emotional Wellness
As a person thinks, so he or she is.
John 8:32, the Bible

Positively Growing My Mind

Reading/audio/video _____

Remember this thought today _____

_____

Beauty appreciated _____

III. My Physical Wellness
Maximum bodily strength and efficiency depend upon three factors:
sleep, exercise, and nutrition.
Dr Martin Shaffer, Life after Stress (New York: Plenum Press, 1982, page 92)

Sleep

Hours:		Quality:					
			Poor	Fair	Moderate	Good	Excellent

Uninterrupted? yes/no _____

Exercise

Aerobic _____

Strength _____

Flexibility _____

Nutrition

Water _____ _____ _____ _____ _____ _____ _____
(check mark per 8 oz.)

Food

Breakfast _____

Snack _____

Lunch _____

Snack _____

Dinner _____

Snack _____

Vitamins/supplements _____

_____

IV. My Social/Relational Wellness

Love is not like other resources.... The more it is used, the more its supply increases.
Dr. Richard Swenson, Margin (Colorado Springs: Navpress, 1992, page 240)

Growing Positive Relationships

Face-to-face with others _____

_____

_____

Phone calls/ written words (email/letters) _____

_____

_____

_____

_____

Purposeful, positive actions I give to others today: _____

_____

_____

_____

_____

_____

_____

What I liked about today/What I didn't like and want to change: _____

_____

_____

_____

_____

_____

Balanced Parenting
✍ My Compass
Day 3

Date:_____

I. My Spiritual Wellness
You will know the truth, and the truth will set you free.
John 8:32, the Bible

Prayer

Contemplating God _____
_____

God, I need to make things right with you with _____
_____

Thank you, God, for _____
_____

God, I need your guidance and help for _____
_____

I ask for wisdom for _____
_____

Reading/Thought for Today
_____
_____

II. My Mental and Emotional Wellness
As a person thinks, so he or she is.
John 8:32, the Bible

Positively Growing My Mind

Reading/audio/video _____

Remember this thought today _____
_____

Beauty appreciated _____

III. My Physical Wellness
Maximum bodily strength and efficiency depend upon three factors:
sleep, exercise, and nutrition.
Dr Martin Shaffer, Life after Stress (New York: Plenum Press, 1982, page 92)

Sleep

Hours:		Quality:					
			Poor	Fair	Moderate	Good	Excellent

Uninterrupted? yes/no _____

Exercise

Aerobic _____

Strength _____

Flexibility _____

Nutrition

Water _____ _____ _____ _____ _____ _____ _____
(check mark per 8 oz.)

Food

Breakfast _____

Snack _____

Lunch _____

Snack _____

Dinner _____

Snack _____

Vitamins/supplements _____

_____

IV. My Social/Relational Wellness

Love is not like other resources.... The more it is used, the more its supply increases.
Dr. Richard Swenson, Margin (Colorado Springs: Navpress, 1992, page 240)

Growing Positive Relationships

Face-to-face with others _____

_____

_____

Phone calls/ written words (email/letters) _____

_____

_____

_____

_____

Purposeful, positive actions I give to others today: _____

_____

_____

_____

_____

_____

_____

What I liked about today/What I didn't like and want to change: _____

_____

_____

_____

_____

_____

Balanced Parenting
✍ My Compass
Day 4

Date: _____

I. My Spiritual Wellness
You will know the truth, and the truth will set you free.
John 8:32, the Bible

Prayer

Contemplating God _____

_____

God, I need to make things right with you with _____

_____

Thank you, God, for _____

_____

God, I need your guidance and help for _____

_____

I ask for wisdom for _____

_____

Reading/Thought for Today

_____

_____

II. My Mental and Emotional Wellness
As a person thinks, so he or she is.
John 8:32, the Bible

Positively Growing My Mind

Reading/audio/video _____

Remember this thought today _____

_____

Beauty appreciated _____

III. My Physical Wellness

Maximum bodily strength and efficiency depend upon three factors:
sleep, exercise, and nutrition.
Dr Martin Shaffer, Life after Stress (New York: Plenum Press, 1982, page 92)

Sleep

Hours:		Quality:		Poor	Fair	Moderate	Good	Excellent

Uninterrupted? yes/no _____

Exercise

Aerobic _____

Strength _____

Flexibility _____

Nutrition

Water _____ _____ _____ _____ _____ _____ _____
(check mark per 8 oz.)

Food

Breakfast _____

Snack _____

Lunch _____

Snack _____

Dinner _____

Snack _____

Vitamins/supplements _____

_____

IV. My Social/Relational Wellness

Love is not like other resources.... The more it is used, the more its supply increases.
Dr. Richard Swenson, Margin (Colorado Springs: Navpress, 1992, page 240)

Growing Positive Relationships

Face-to-face with others _____

_____

_____

Phone calls/ written words (email/letters) _____

_____

_____

_____

_____

Purposeful, positive actions I give to others today: _____

_____

_____

_____

_____

_____

_____

What I liked about today/What I didn't like and want to change: _____

_____

_____

_____

_____

_____

Balanced Parenting
✍ My Compass
Day 5

Date:_____

I. My Spiritual Wellness
You will know the truth, and the truth will set you free.
John 8:32, the Bible

Prayer

Contemplating God _____

_____

God, I need to make things right with you with _____

_____

Thank you, God, for _____

_____

God, I need your guidance and help for _____

_____

I ask for wisdom for _____

_____

Reading/Thought for Today

_____

_____

II. My Mental and Emotional Wellness
As a person thinks, so he or she is.
John 8:32, the Bible

Positively Growing My Mind

Reading/audio/video _____

Remember this thought today _____

_____

Beauty appreciated _____

III. My Physical Wellness

Maximum bodily strength and efficiency depend upon three factors:
sleep, exercise, and nutrition.
Dr Martin Shaffer, Life after Stress (New York: Plenum Press, 1982, page 92)

Sleep

Hours:		Quality:					
			Poor	Fair	Moderate	Good	Excellent

Uninterrupted? yes/no _____

Exercise

Aerobic _____

Strength _____

Flexibility _____

Nutrition

Water _____ _____ _____ _____ _____ _____ _____
(check mark per 8 oz.)

Food

Breakfast _____

Snack _____

Lunch _____

Snack _____

Dinner _____

Snack _____

Vitamins/supplements _____

_____

IV. My Social/Relational Wellness

Love is not like other resources.... The more it is used, the more its supply increases.
Dr. Richard Swenson, Margin (Colorado Springs: Navpress, 1992, page 240)

Growing Positive Relationships

Face-to-face with others _____

_____

_____

Phone calls/ written words (email/letters) _____

_____

_____

_____

_____

Purposeful, positive actions I give to others today: _____

_____

_____

_____

_____

_____

_____

What I liked about today/What I didn't like and want to change: _____

_____

_____

_____

_____

_____

Balanced Parenting
✍ My Compass
Day 6

Date:_____

I. My Spiritual Wellness
You will know the truth, and the truth will set you free.
John 8:32, the Bible

Prayer

Contemplating God _____

_____

God, I need to make things right with you with _____

_____

Thank you, God, for _____

_____

God, I need your guidance and help for _____

_____

I ask for wisdom for _____

_____

Reading/Thought for Today

_____

_____

II. My Mental and Emotional Wellness
As a person thinks, so he or she is.
John 8:32, the Bible

Positively Growing My Mind

Reading/audio/video _____

Remember this thought today _____

_____

Beauty appreciated _____

III. My Physical Wellness
Maximum bodily strength and efficiency depend upon three factors:
sleep, exercise, and nutrition.
Dr Martin Shaffer, Life after Stress (New York: Plenum Press, 1982, page 92)

Sleep

Hours:		Quality:	Poor	Fair	Moderate	Good	Excellent

Uninterrupted? yes/no _____

Exercise

Aerobic _____

Strength _____

Flexibility _____

Nutrition

Water _____ _____ _____ _____ _____ _____ _____
(check mark per 8 oz.)

Food

Breakfast _____

Snack _____

Lunch _____

Snack _____

Dinner _____

Snack _____

Vitamins/supplements _____

_____

IV. My Social/Relational Wellness

Love is not like other resources.... The more it is used, the more its supply increases.
Dr. Richard Swenson, Margin (Colorado Springs: Navpress, 1992, page 240)

Growing Positive Relationships

Face-to-face with others _____

_____

_____

Phone calls/ written words (email/letters) _____

_____

_____

_____

_____

Purposeful, positive actions I give to others today: _____

_____

_____

_____

_____

_____

_____

What I liked about today/What I didn't like and want to change: _____

_____

_____

_____

_____

_____

Balanced Parenting
✍ My Compass
Day 7

Date:_____

I. My Spiritual Wellness
You will know the truth, and the truth will set you free.
John 8:32, the Bible

Prayer

Contemplating God _____

_____

God, I need to make things right with you with _____

_____

Thank you, God, for _____

_____

God, I need your guidance and help for _____

_____

I ask for wisdom for _____

_____

Reading/Thought for Today

_____

_____

II. My Mental and Emotional Wellness
As a person thinks, so he or she is.
John 8:32, the Bible

Positively Growing My Mind

Reading/audio/video _____

Remember this thought today _____

_____

Beauty appreciated _____

III. My Physical Wellness
Maximum bodily strength and efficiency depend upon three factors:
sleep, exercise, and nutrition.
Dr Martin Shaffer, Life after Stress (New York: Plenum Press, 1982, page 92)

Sleep

Hours:		Quality:					
			Poor	Fair	Moderate	Good	Excellent

Uninterrupted? yes/no _____

Exercise

Aerobic _____

Strength _____

Flexibility _____

Nutrition

Water _____ _____ _____ _____ _____ _____ _____
                     (check mark per 8 oz.)

Food

Breakfast _____

Snack _____

Lunch _____

Snack _____

Dinner _____

Snack _____

Vitamins/supplements _____

_____

IV. My Social/Relational Wellness

Love is not like other resources.... The more it is used, the more its supply increases.
Dr. Richard Swenson, Margin (Colorado Springs: Navpress, 1992, page 240)

Growing Positive Relationships

Face-to-face with others _____

_____

_____

Phone calls/ written words (email/letters) _____

_____

_____

_____

_____

Purposeful, positive actions I give to others today: _____

_____

_____

_____

_____

_____

_____

What I liked about today/What I didn't like and want to change: _____

_____

_____

_____

_____

_____

Balanced Parenting
✍ My Compass
Day 8

Date:_____

I. My Spiritual Wellness

You will know the truth, and the truth will set you free.
John 8:32, the Bible

Prayer

Contemplating God _____

_____

God, I need to make things right with you with _____

_____

Thank you, God, for _____

_____

God, I need your guidance and help for _____

_____

I ask for wisdom for _____

_____

Reading/Thought for Today

_____

_____

II. My Mental and Emotional Wellness

As a person thinks, so he or she is.
John 8:32, the Bible

Positively Growing My Mind

Reading/audio/video _____

Remember this thought today _____

_____

Beauty appreciated _____

III. My Physical Wellness
Maximum bodily strength and efficiency depend upon three factors:
sleep, exercise, and nutrition.
Dr Martin Shaffer, Life after Stress (New York: Plenum Press, 1982, page 92)

Sleep

Hours:		Quality:					
			Poor	Fair	Moderate	Good	Excellent

Uninterrupted? yes/no _____

Exercise

Aerobic _____

Strength _____

Flexibility _____

Nutrition

Water _____ _____ _____ _____ _____ _____ _____
(check mark per 8 oz.)

Food

Breakfast _____

Snack _____

Lunch _____

Snack _____

Dinner _____

Snack _____

Vitamins/supplements _____

_____

IV. My Social/Relational Wellness

Love is not like other resources.... The more it is used, the more its supply increases.
Dr. Richard Swenson, Margin (Colorado Springs: Navpress, 1992, page 240)

Growing Positive Relationships

Face-to-face with others _____

_____

_____

Phone calls/ written words (email/letters) _____

_____

_____

_____

_____

Purposeful, positive actions I give to others today: _____

_____

_____

_____

_____

_____

_____

What I liked about today/What I didn't like and want to change: _____

_____

_____

_____

_____

_____

Balanced Parenting
✍ My Compass
Day 9

Date:_____

I. My Spiritual Wellness
You will know the truth, and the truth will set you free.
John 8:32, the Bible

Prayer

Contemplating God _____

_____

God, I need to make things right with you with _____

_____

Thank you, God, for _____

_____

God, I need your guidance and help for _____

_____

I ask for wisdom for _____

_____

Reading/Thought for Today

_____

_____

II. My Mental and Emotional Wellness
As a person thinks, so he or she is.
John 8:32, the Bible

Positively Growing My Mind

Reading/audio/video _____

Remember this thought today _____

_____

Beauty appreciated _____

III. My Physical Wellness
Maximum bodily strength and efficiency depend upon three factors:
sleep, exercise, and nutrition.
Dr Martin Shaffer, Life after Stress (New York: Plenum Press, 1982, page 92)

Sleep

Hours:		Quality:					
			Poor	Fair	Moderate	Good	Excellent

Uninterrupted? yes/no _____

Exercise

Aerobic _____

Strength _____

Flexibility _____

Nutrition

Water _____ _____ _____ _____ _____ _____ _____
(check mark per 8 oz.)

Food

Breakfast _____

Snack _____

Lunch _____

Snack _____

Dinner _____

Snack _____

Vitamins/supplements _____

_____

IV. My Social/Relational Wellness

Love is not like other resources.... The more it is used, the more its supply increases.
Dr. Richard Swenson, Margin (Colorado Springs: Navpress, 1992, page 240)

Growing Positive Relationships

Face-to-face with others _____

_____

_____

Phone calls/ written words (email/letters) _____

_____

_____

_____

_____

Purposeful, positive actions I give to others today: _____

_____

_____

_____

_____

_____

_____

What I liked about today/What I didn't like and want to change: _____

_____

_____

_____

_____

_____

Balanced Parenting
✍ My Compass
Day 10

Date:_____

I. My Spiritual Wellness

You will know the truth, and the truth will set you free.
John 8:32, the Bible

Prayer

Contemplating God _____

_____

God, I need to make things right with you with _____

_____

Thank you, God, for _____

_____

God, I need your guidance and help for _____

_____

I ask for wisdom for _____

_____

Reading/Thought for Today

_____

_____

II. My Mental and Emotional Wellness

As a person thinks, so he or she is.
John 8:32, the Bible

Positively Growing My Mind

Reading/audio/video _____

Remember this thought today _____

_____

Beauty appreciated _____

III. My Physical Wellness
Maximum bodily strength and efficiency depend upon three factors:
sleep, exercise, and nutrition.
Dr Martin Shaffer, Life after Stress (New York: Plenum Press, 1982, page 92)

Sleep

Hours:		Quality:					
			Poor	Fair	Moderate	Good	Excellent

Uninterrupted? yes/no _____

Exercise

Aerobic _____

Strength _____

Flexibility _____

Nutrition

Water _____ _____ _____ _____ _____ _____ _____
(check mark per 8 oz.)

Food

Breakfast _____

Snack _____

Lunch _____

Snack _____

Dinner _____

Snack _____

Vitamins/supplements _____

_____

IV. My Social/Relational Wellness

Love is not like other resources.... The more it is used, the more its supply increases.
Dr. Richard Swenson, Margin (Colorado Springs: Navpress, 1992, page 240)

Growing Positive Relationships

Face-to-face with others _____

_____

_____

Phone calls/ written words (email/letters) _____

_____

_____

_____

_____

Purposeful, positive actions I give to others today: _____

_____

_____

_____

_____

_____

_____

_____

What I liked about today/What I didn't like and want to change: _____

_____

_____

_____

_____

_____

Balanced Parenting
✍ My Compass
Day 11

Date:_____

I. My Spiritual Wellness
You will know the truth, and the truth will set you free.
John 8:32, the Bible

Prayer

Contemplating God _____

_____

God, I need to make things right with you with _____

_____

Thank you, God, for _____

_____

God, I need your guidance and help for _____

_____

I ask for wisdom for _____

_____

Reading/Thought for Today

_____

_____

II. My Mental and Emotional Wellness
As a person thinks, so he or she is.
John 8:32, the Bible

Positively Growing My Mind

Reading/audio/video _____

Remember this thought today _____

_____

Beauty appreciated _____

III. My Physical Wellness
Maximum bodily strength and efficiency depend upon three factors:
sleep, exercise, and nutrition.
Dr Martin Shaffer, Life after Stress (New York: Plenum Press, 1982, page 92)

Sleep

Hours:		Quality:	Poor	Fair	Moderate	Good	Excellent

Uninterrupted? yes/no _____

Exercise

Aerobic _____

Strength _____

Flexibility _____

Nutrition

Water _____ _____ _____ _____ _____ _____ _____
(check mark per 8 oz.)

Food

Breakfast _____

Snack _____

Lunch _____

Snack _____

Dinner _____

Snack _____

Vitamins/supplements _____

_____

IV. My Social/Relational Wellness

Love is not like other resources.... The more it is used, the more its supply increases.
Dr. Richard Swenson, Margin (Colorado Springs: Navpress, 1992, page 240)

Growing Positive Relationships

Face-to-face with others _____

_____

_____

Phone calls/ written words (email/letters) _____

_____

_____

_____

_____

Purposeful, positive actions I give to others today: _____

_____

_____

_____

_____

_____

_____

What I liked about today/What I didn't like and want to change: _____

_____

_____

_____

_____

_____

Balanced Parenting
✍ My Compass
Day 12

Date:_____

I. My Spiritual Wellness
You will know the truth, and the truth will set you free.
John 8:32, the Bible

Prayer

Contemplating God _____

_____

God, I need to make things right with you with _____

_____

Thank you, God, for _____

_____

God, I need your guidance and help for _____

_____

I ask for wisdom for _____

_____

Reading/Thought for Today

_____

_____

II. My Mental and Emotional Wellness
As a person thinks, so he or she is.
John 8:32, the Bible

Positively Growing My Mind

Reading/audio/video _____

Remember this thought today _____

_____

Beauty appreciated _____

III. My Physical Wellness
Maximum bodily strength and efficiency depend upon three factors:
sleep, exercise, and nutrition.
Dr Martin Shaffer, Life after Stress (New York: Plenum Press, 1982, page 92)

Sleep

Hours:	Quality:					
		Poor	Fair	Moderate	Good	Excellent

Uninterrupted? yes/no _____

Exercise

Aerobic _____

Strength _____

Flexibility _____

Nutrition

Water _____ _____ _____ _____ _____ _____ _____
(check mark per 8 oz.)

Food

Breakfast _____

Snack _____

Lunch _____

Snack _____

Dinner _____

Snack _____

Vitamins/supplements _____

_____

IV. My Social/Relational Wellness

Love is not like other resources.... The more it is used, the more its supply increases.
Dr. Richard Swenson, Margin (Colorado Springs: Navpress, 1992, page 240)

Growing Positive Relationships

Face-to-face with others _____

_____

_____

Phone calls/ written words (email/letters) _____

_____

_____

_____

_____

Purposeful, positive actions I give to others today: _____

_____

_____

_____

_____

_____

_____

What I liked about today/What I didn't like and want to change: _____

_____

_____

_____

_____

_____

Balanced Parenting
✍ My Compass
Day 13

Date:_____

I. My Spiritual Wellness
You will know the truth, and the truth will set you free.
John 8:32, the Bible

Prayer

Contemplating God _____

_____

God, I need to make things right with you with _____

_____

Thank you, God, for _____

_____

God, I need your guidance and help for _____

_____

I ask for wisdom for _____

_____

Reading/Thought for Today

_____

_____

II. My Mental and Emotional Wellness
As a person thinks, so he or she is.
John 8:32, the Bible

Positively Growing My Mind

Reading/audio/video _____

Remember this thought today _____

_____

Beauty appreciated _____

III. My Physical Wellness

Maximum bodily strength and efficiency depend upon three factors:
sleep, exercise, and nutrition.
Dr Martin Shaffer, Life after Stress (New York: Plenum Press, 1982, page 92)

Sleep

Hours:		Quality:					
			Poor	Fair	Moderate	Good	Excellent

Uninterrupted? yes/no _____

Exercise

Aerobic _____

Strength _____

Flexibility _____

Nutrition

Water _____ _____ _____ _____ _____ _____ _____
(check mark per 8 oz.)

Food

Breakfast _____

Snack _____

Lunch _____

Snack _____

Dinner _____

Snack _____

Vitamins/supplements _____

_____

IV. My Social/Relational Wellness

Love is not like other resources.... The more it is used, the more its supply increases.
Dr. Richard Swenson, Margin (Colorado Springs: Navpress, 1992, page 240)

Growing Positive Relationships

Face-to-face with others _____

_____

_____

Phone calls/ written words (email/letters) _____

_____

_____

_____

_____

Purposeful, positive actions I give to others today: _____

_____

_____

_____

_____

_____

_____

What I liked about today/What I didn't like and want to change: _____

_____

_____

_____

_____

_____

Balanced Parenting
✍ My Compass
Day 14

Date:_____

I. My Spiritual Wellness
You will know the truth, and the truth will set you free.
John 8:32, the Bible

Prayer

Contemplating God _____

_____

God, I need to make things right with you with _____

_____

Thank you, God, for _____

_____

God, I need your guidance and help for _____

_____

I ask for wisdom for _____

_____

Reading/Thought for Today

_____

_____

II. My Mental and Emotional Wellness
As a person thinks, so he or she is.
John 8:32, the Bible

Positively Growing My Mind

Reading/audio/video _____

Remember this thought today _____

_____

Beauty appreciated _____

III. My Physical Wellness

Maximum bodily strength and efficiency depend upon three factors:
sleep, exercise, and nutrition.
Dr Martin Shaffer, Life after Stress (New York: Plenum Press, 1982, page 92)

Sleep

Hours:		Quality:		Poor	Fair	Moderate	Good	Excellent

Uninterrupted? yes/no _____

Exercise

Aerobic _____

Strength _____

Flexibility _____

Nutrition

Water _____ _____ _____ _____ _____ _____ _____
(check mark per 8 oz.)

Food

Breakfast _____

Snack _____

Lunch _____

Snack _____

Dinner _____

Snack _____

Vitamins/supplements _____

_____

IV. My Social/Relational Wellness

Love is not like other resources.... The more it is used, the more its supply increases.
Dr. Richard Swenson, Margin (Colorado Springs: Navpress, 1992, page 240)

Growing Positive Relationships

Face-to-face with others _____

_____

_____

Phone calls/ written words (email/letters) _____

_____

_____

_____

_____

Purposeful, positive actions I give to others today: _____

_____

_____

_____

_____

_____

_____

What I liked about today/What I didn't like and want to change: _____

_____

_____

_____

_____

_____

Balanced Parenting
✍ My Compass
Day 15

Date: _____

I. My Spiritual Wellness
You will know the truth, and the truth will set you free.
John 8:32, the Bible

Prayer

Contemplating God _____

_____

God, I need to make things right with you with _____

_____

Thank you, God, for _____

_____

God, I need your guidance and help for _____

_____

I ask for wisdom for _____

_____

Reading/Thought for Today

_____

_____

II. My Mental and Emotional Wellness
As a person thinks, so he or she is.
John 8:32, the Bible

Positively Growing My Mind

Reading/audio/video _____

Remember this thought today _____

_____

Beauty appreciated _____

III. My Physical Wellness

Maximum bodily strength and efficiency depend upon three factors:
sleep, exercise, and nutrition.
Dr Martin Shaffer, Life after Stress (New York: Plenum Press, 1982, page 92)

Sleep

Hours:		Quality:	Poor	Fair	Moderate	Good	Excellent

Uninterrupted? yes/no _____

Exercise

Aerobic _____

Strength _____

Flexibility _____

Nutrition

Water _____ _____ _____ _____ _____ _____ _____
(check mark per 8 oz.)

Food

Breakfast _____

Snack _____

Lunch _____

Snack _____

Dinner _____

Snack _____

Vitamins/supplements _____

_____

IV. My Social/Relational Wellness

Love is not like other resources.... The more it is used, the more its supply increases.
Dr. Richard Swenson, Margin (Colorado Springs: Navpress, 1992, page 240)

Growing Positive Relationships

Face-to-face with others _____

_____

_____

Phone calls/ written words (email/letters) _____

_____

_____

_____

_____

Purposeful, positive actions I give to others today: _____

_____

_____

_____

_____

_____

_____

What I liked about today/What I didn't like and want to change: _____

_____

_____

_____

_____

_____

Balanced Parenting
✍ My Compass
Day 16

Date:_____

I. My Spiritual Wellness
You will know the truth, and the truth will set you free.
John 8:32, the Bible

Prayer

Contemplating God _____

_____

God, I need to make things right with you with _____

_____

Thank you, God, for _____

_____

God, I need your guidance and help for _____

_____

I ask for wisdom for _____

_____

Reading/Thought for Today

_____

_____

II. My Mental and Emotional Wellness
As a person thinks, so he or she is.
John 8:32, the Bible

Positively Growing My Mind

Reading/audio/video _____

Remember this thought today _____

_____

Beauty appreciated _____

III. My Physical Wellness
Maximum bodily strength and efficiency depend upon three factors:
sleep, exercise, and nutrition.
Dr Martin Shaffer, Life after Stress (New York: Plenum Press, 1982, page 92)

Sleep

Hours:		Quality:					
			Poor	Fair	Moderate	Good	Excellent

Uninterrupted? yes/no _____

Exercise

Aerobic _____

Strength _____

Flexibility _____

Nutrition

Water _____ _____ _____ _____ _____ _____ _____
(check mark per 8 oz.)

Food

Breakfast _____

Snack _____

Lunch _____

Snack _____

Dinner _____

Snack _____

Vitamins/supplements _____

_____

IV. My Social/Relational Wellness

Love is not like other resources.... The more it is used, the more its supply increases.
Dr. Richard Swenson, Margin (Colorado Springs: Navpress, 1992, page 240)

Growing Positive Relationships

Face-to-face with others _____

_____

_____

Phone calls/ written words (email/letters) _____

_____

_____

_____

_____

Purposeful, positive actions I give to others today: _____

_____

_____

_____

_____

_____

_____

What I liked about today/What I didn't like and want to change: _____

_____

_____

_____

_____

_____

Balanced Parenting
✍ My Compass
Day 17

Date:_____

I. My Spiritual Wellness
You will know the truth, and the truth will set you free.
John 8:32, the Bible

Prayer

Contemplating God _____

_____

God, I need to make things right with you with _____

_____

Thank you, God, for _____

_____

God, I need your guidance and help for _____

_____

I ask for wisdom for _____

_____

Reading/Thought for Today

_____

_____

II. My Mental and Emotional Wellness
As a person thinks, so he or she is.
John 8:32, the Bible

Positively Growing My Mind

Reading/audio/video _____

Remember this thought today _____

_____

Beauty appreciated _____

III. My Physical Wellness

Maximum bodily strength and efficiency depend upon three factors:
sleep, exercise, and nutrition.

Dr Martin Shaffer, Life after Stress (New York: Plenum Press, 1982, page 92)

Sleep

Hours:		Quality:					
			Poor	Fair	Moderate	Good	Excellent

Uninterrupted? yes/no _____

Exercise

Aerobic _____

Strength _____

Flexibility _____

Nutrition

Water _____ _____ _____ _____ _____ _____ _____
(check mark per 8 oz.)

Food

Breakfast _____

Snack _____

Lunch _____

Snack _____

Dinner _____

Snack _____

Vitamins/supplements _____

_____

IV. My Social/Relational Wellness

Love is not like other resources.... The more it is used, the more its supply increases.
Dr. Richard Swenson, Margin (Colorado Springs: Navpress, 1992, page 240)

Growing Positive Relationships

Face-to-face with others _____

_____

_____

Phone calls/ written words (email/letters) _____

_____

_____

_____

_____

Purposeful, positive actions I give to others today: _____

_____

_____

_____

_____

_____

_____

What I liked about today/What I didn't like and want to change: _____

_____

_____

_____

_____

_____

Balanced Parenting
✍ My Compass
Day 18

Date:_____

I. My Spiritual Wellness
You will know the truth, and the truth will set you free.
John 8:32, the Bible

Prayer

Contemplating God _____

_____

God, I need to make things right with you with _____

_____

Thank you, God, for _____

_____

God, I need your guidance and help for _____

_____

I ask for wisdom for _____

_____

Reading/Thought for Today

_____

_____

II. My Mental and Emotional Wellness
As a person thinks, so he or she is.
John 8:32, the Bible

Positively Growing My Mind

Reading/audio/video _____

Remember this thought today _____

_____

Beauty appreciated _____

III. My Physical Wellness
Maximum bodily strength and efficiency depend upon three factors:
sleep, exercise, and nutrition.
Dr Martin Shaffer, Life after Stress (New York: Plenum Press, 1982, page 92)

Sleep

Hours:		Quality:					
			Poor	Fair	Moderate	Good	Excellent

Uninterrupted? yes/no _____

Exercise

Aerobic _____

Strength _____

Flexibility _____

Nutrition

Water _____ _____ _____ _____ _____ _____ _____
(check mark per 8 oz.)

Food

Breakfast _____

Snack _____

Lunch _____

Snack _____

Dinner _____

Snack _____

Vitamins/supplements _____

_____

IV. My Social/Relational Wellness

Love is not like other resources.... The more it is used, the more its supply increases.
Dr. Richard Swenson, Margin (Colorado Springs: Navpress, 1992, page 240)

Growing Positive Relationships

Face-to-face with others _____

_____

_____

Phone calls/ written words (email/letters) _____

_____

_____

_____

_____

Purposeful, positive actions I give to others today: _____

_____

_____

_____

_____

_____

_____

What I liked about today/What I didn't like and want to change: _____

_____

_____

_____

_____

_____

Balanced Parenting
✍ My Compass
Day 19

Date:_____

I. My Spiritual Wellness
You will know the truth, and the truth will set you free.
John 8:32, the Bible

Prayer

Contemplating God _____

_____

God, I need to make things right with you with _____

_____

Thank you, God, for _____

_____

God, I need your guidance and help for _____

_____

I ask for wisdom for _____

_____

Reading/Thought for Today

_____

_____

II. My Mental and Emotional Wellness
As a person thinks, so he or she is.
John 8:32, the Bible

Positively Growing My Mind

Reading/audio/video _____

Remember this thought today _____

_____

Beauty appreciated _____

III. My Physical Wellness

Maximum bodily strength and efficiency depend upon three factors:
sleep, exercise, and nutrition.
Dr Martin Shaffer, Life after Stress (New York: Plenum Press, 1982, page 92)

Sleep

Hours:		Quality:					
			Poor	Fair	Moderate	Good	Excellent

Uninterrupted? yes/no _____

Exercise

Aerobic _____

Strength _____

Flexibility _____

Nutrition

Water _____ _____ _____ _____ _____ _____ _____
(check mark per 8 oz.)

Food

Breakfast _____

Snack _____

Lunch _____

Snack _____

Dinner _____

Snack _____

Vitamins/supplements _____

_____

IV. My Social/Relational Wellness
Love is not like other resources.... The more it is used, the more its supply increases.
Dr. Richard Swenson, Margin (Colorado Springs: Navpress, 1992, page 240)

Growing Positive Relationships

Face-to-face with others _____

_____

_____

Phone calls/ written words (email/letters) _____

_____

_____

_____

_____

Purposeful, positive actions I give to others today: _____

_____

_____

_____

_____

_____

_____

What I liked about today/What I didn't like and want to change: _____

_____

_____

_____

_____

_____

Balanced Parenting
✍ My Compass
Day 20

Date:_____

I. My Spiritual Wellness
You will know the truth, and the truth will set you free.
John 8:32, the Bible

Prayer

Contemplating God _____

_____

God, I need to make things right with you with _____

_____

Thank you, God, for _____

_____

God, I need your guidance and help for _____

_____

I ask for wisdom for _____

_____

Reading/Thought for Today

_____

_____

II. My Mental and Emotional Wellness
As a person thinks, so he or she is.
John 8:32, the Bible

Positively Growing My Mind

Reading/audio/video _____

Remember this thought today _____

_____

Beauty appreciated _____

III. My Physical Wellness

Maximum bodily strength and efficiency depend upon three factors:
sleep, exercise, and nutrition.
Dr Martin Shaffer, Life after Stress (New York: Plenum Press, 1982, page 92)

Sleep

Hours:		Quality:					
			Poor	Fair	Moderate	Good	Excellent

Uninterrupted? yes/no _____

Exercise

Aerobic _____

Strength _____

Flexibility _____

Nutrition

Water _____ _____ _____ _____ _____ _____ _____
(check mark per 8 oz.)

Food

Breakfast _____

Snack _____

Lunch _____

Snack _____

Dinner _____

Snack _____

Vitamins/supplements _____

_____

IV. My Social/Relational Wellness

Love is not like other resources.... The more it is used, the more its supply increases.
Dr. Richard Swenson, Margin (Colorado Springs: Navpress, 1992, page 240)

Growing Positive Relationships

Face-to-face with others _____

_____

_____

Phone calls/ written words (email/letters) _____

_____

_____

_____

_____

Purposeful, positive actions I give to others today: _____

_____

_____

_____

_____

_____

_____

_____

What I liked about today/What I didn't like and want to change: _____

_____

_____

_____

_____

_____

Balanced Parenting
✐ My Compass
Day 21

Date:_____

I. My Spiritual Wellness
You will know the truth, and the truth will set you free.
John 8:32, the Bible

Prayer

Contemplating God _____

_____

God, I need to make things right with you with _____

_____

Thank you, God, for _____

_____

God, I need your guidance and help for _____

_____

I ask for wisdom for _____

_____

Reading/Thought for Today

_____

_____

II. My Mental and Emotional Wellness
As a person thinks, so he or she is.
John 8:32, the Bible

Positively Growing My Mind

Reading/audio/video _____

Remember this thought today _____

_____

Beauty appreciated _____

III. My Physical Wellness

Maximum bodily strength and efficiency depend upon three factors:
sleep, exercise, and nutrition.
Dr Martin Shaffer, Life after Stress (New York: Plenum Press, 1982, page 92)

Sleep

Hours:		Quality:					
			Poor	Fair	Moderate	Good	Excellent

Uninterrupted? yes/no _____

Exercise

Aerobic _____

Strength _____

Flexibility _____

Nutrition

Water _____ _____ _____ _____ _____ _____ _____
(check mark per 8 oz.)

Food

Breakfast _____

Snack _____

Lunch _____

Snack _____

Dinner _____

Snack _____

Vitamins/supplements _____

_____

IV. My Social/Relational Wellness

Love is not like other resources.... The more it is used, the more its supply increases.
Dr. Richard Swenson, Margin (Colorado Springs: Navpress, 1992, page 240)

Growing Positive Relationships

Face-to-face with others _____

_____

_____

Phone calls/ written words (email/letters) _____

_____

_____

_____

_____

Purposeful, positive actions I give to others today: _____

_____

_____

_____

_____

_____

_____

What I liked about today/What I didn't like and want to change: _____

_____

_____

_____

_____

_____

Balanced Parenting
✍ My Compass
Day 22

Date:_____

I. My Spiritual Wellness
You will know the truth, and the truth will set you free.
John 8:32, the Bible

Prayer

Contemplating God _____

_____

God, I need to make things right with you with _____

_____

Thank you, God, for _____

_____

God, I need your guidance and help for _____

_____

I ask for wisdom for _____

_____

Reading/Thought for Today

_____

_____

II. My Mental and Emotional Wellness
As a person thinks, so he or she is.
John 8:32, the Bible

Positively Growing My Mind

Reading/audio/video _____

Remember this thought today _____

_____

Beauty appreciated _____

III. My Physical Wellness
Maximum bodily strength and efficiency depend upon three factors:
sleep, exercise, and nutrition.
Dr Martin Shaffer, Life after Stress (New York: Plenum Press, 1982, page 92)

Sleep

Hours:		Quality:					
			Poor	Fair	Moderate	Good	Excellent

Uninterrupted? yes/no _____

Exercise

Aerobic _____

Strength _____

Flexibility _____

Nutrition

Water _____ _____ _____ _____ _____ _____ _____
(check mark per 8 oz.)

Food

Breakfast _____

Snack _____

Lunch _____

Snack _____

Dinner _____

Snack _____

Vitamins/supplements _____

_____

IV. My Social/Relational Wellness
Love is not like other resources.... The more it is used, the more its supply increases.
Dr. Richard Swenson, Margin (Colorado Springs: Navpress, 1992, page 240)

Growing Positive Relationships

Face-to-face with others _____

_____

_____

Phone calls/ written words (email/letters) _____

_____

_____

_____

_____

Purposeful, positive actions I give to others today: _____

_____

_____

_____

_____

_____

_____

What I liked about today/What I didn't like and want to change: _____

_____

_____

_____

_____

_____

Balanced Parenting
✍ My Compass
Day 23

Date:_____

I. My Spiritual Wellness
You will know the truth, and the truth will set you free.
John 8:32, the Bible

Prayer

Contemplating God _____

_____

God, I need to make things right with you with _____

_____

Thank you, God, for _____

_____

God, I need your guidance and help for _____

_____

I ask for wisdom for _____

_____

Reading/Thought for Today

_____

_____

II. My Mental and Emotional Wellness
As a person thinks, so he or she is.
John 8:32, the Bible

Positively Growing My Mind

Reading/audio/video _____

Remember this thought today _____

_____

Beauty appreciated _____

III. My Physical Wellness

Maximum bodily strength and efficiency depend upon three factors:
sleep, exercise, and nutrition.
Dr Martin Shaffer, Life after Stress (New York: Plenum Press, 1982, page 92)

Sleep

Hours:		Quality:					
			Poor	Fair	Moderate	Good	Excellent

Uninterrupted? yes/no _____

Exercise

Aerobic _____

Strength _____

Flexibility _____

Nutrition

Water _____ _____ _____ _____ _____ _____ _____
(check mark per 8 oz.)

Food

Breakfast _____

Snack _____

Lunch _____

Snack _____

Dinner _____

Snack _____

Vitamins/supplements _____

_____

IV. My Social/Relational Wellness

Love is not like other resources.... The more it is used, the more its supply increases.
Dr. Richard Swenson, Margin (Colorado Springs: Navpress, 1992, page 240)

Growing Positive Relationships

Face-to-face with others _____

_____

_____

Phone calls/ written words (email/letters) _____

_____

_____

_____

_____

Purposeful, positive actions I give to others today: _____

_____

_____

_____

_____

_____

_____

What I liked about today/What I didn't like and want to change: _____

_____

_____

_____

_____

_____

Balanced Parenting
✍ My Compass
Day 24

Date:_____

I. My Spiritual Wellness
You will know the truth, and the truth will set you free.
John 8:32, the Bible

Prayer

Contemplating God _____

_____

God, I need to make things right with you with _____

_____

Thank you, God, for _____

_____

God, I need your guidance and help for _____

_____

I ask for wisdom for _____

_____

Reading/Thought for Today

_____

_____

II. My Mental and Emotional Wellness
As a person thinks, so he or she is.
John 8:32, the Bible

Positively Growing My Mind

Reading/audio/video _____

Remember this thought today _____

_____

Beauty appreciated _____

III. My Physical Wellness
Maximum bodily strength and efficiency depend upon three factors:
sleep, exercise, and nutrition.
Dr Martin Shaffer, Life after Stress (New York: Plenum Press, 1982, page 92)

Sleep

Hours:		Quality:	Poor	Fair	Moderate	Good	Excellent

Uninterrupted? yes/no _____

Exercise

Aerobic _____

Strength _____

Flexibility _____

Nutrition

Water _____ _____ _____ _____ _____ _____ _____
(check mark per 8 oz.)

Food

Breakfast _____

Snack _____

Lunch _____

Snack _____

Dinner _____

Snack _____

Vitamins/supplements _____

_____

IV. My Social/Relational Wellness

Love is not like other resources.... The more it is used, the more its supply increases.
Dr. Richard Swenson, Margin (Colorado Springs: Navpress, 1992, page 240)

Growing Positive Relationships

Face-to-face with others _____

_____

_____

Phone calls/ written words (email/letters) _____

_____

_____

_____

_____

Purposeful, positive actions I give to others today: _____

_____

_____

_____

_____

_____

_____

_____

What I liked about today/What I didn't like and want to change: _____

_____

_____

_____

_____

_____

Balanced Parenting
✍ My Compass
Day 25

Date:_____

I. My Spiritual Wellness
You will know the truth, and the truth will set you free.
John 8:32, the Bible

Prayer

Contemplating God _____

_____

God, I need to make things right with you with _____

_____

Thank you, God, for _____

_____

God, I need your guidance and help for _____

_____

I ask for wisdom for _____

_____

Reading/Thought for Today

_____

_____

II. My Mental and Emotional Wellness
As a person thinks, so he or she is.
John 8:32, the Bible

Positively Growing My Mind

Reading/audio/video _____

Remember this thought today _____

_____

Beauty appreciated _____

III. My Physical Wellness

Maximum bodily strength and efficiency depend upon three factors:
sleep, exercise, and nutrition.
Dr Martin Shaffer, Life after Stress (New York: Plenum Press, 1982, page 92)

Sleep

Hours:		Quality:					
			Poor	Fair	Moderate	Good	Excellent

Uninterrupted? yes/no _____

Exercise

Aerobic _____

Strength _____

Flexibility _____

Nutrition

Water _____ _____ _____ _____ _____ _____ _____
(check mark per 8 oz.)

Food

Breakfast _____

Snack _____

Lunch _____

Snack _____

Dinner _____

Snack _____

Vitamins/supplements _____

_____

IV. My Social/Relational Wellness
Love is not like other resources.... The more it is used, the more its supply increases.
Dr. Richard Swenson, Margin (Colorado Springs: Navpress, 1992, page 240)

Growing Positive Relationships

Face-to-face with others _____

_____

_____

Phone calls/ written words (email/letters) _____

_____

_____

_____

_____

Purposeful, positive actions I give to others today: _____

_____

_____

_____

_____

_____

_____

What I liked about today/What I didn't like and want to change: _____

_____

_____

_____

_____

_____

Balanced Parenting
✍ My Compass
Day 26

Date:_____

I. My Spiritual Wellness
You will know the truth, and the truth will set you free.
John 8:32, the Bible

Prayer

Contemplating God _____

_____

God, I need to make things right with you with _____

_____

Thank you, God, for _____

_____

God, I need your guidance and help for _____

_____

I ask for wisdom for _____

_____

Reading/Thought for Today

_____

_____

II. My Mental and Emotional Wellness
As a person thinks, so he or she is.
John 8:32, the Bible

Positively Growing My Mind

Reading/audio/video _____

Remember this thought today _____

_____

Beauty appreciated _____

III. My Physical Wellness
Maximum bodily strength and efficiency depend upon three factors:
sleep, exercise, and nutrition.
Dr Martin Shaffer, Life after Stress (New York: Plenum Press, 1982, page 92)

Sleep

Hours:		Quality:					
			Poor	Fair	Moderate	Good	Excellent

Uninterrupted? yes/no _____

Exercise

Aerobic _____

Strength _____

Flexibility _____

Nutrition

Water _____ _____ _____ _____ _____ _____ _____
(check mark per 8 oz.)

Food

Breakfast _____

Snack _____

Lunch _____

Snack _____

Dinner _____

Snack _____

Vitamins/supplements _____

_____

IV. My Social/Relational Wellness

Love is not like other resources.... The more it is used, the more its supply increases.
Dr. Richard Swenson, Margin (Colorado Springs: Navpress, 1992, page 240)

Growing Positive Relationships

Face-to-face with others _____

_____

_____

Phone calls/ written words (email/letters) _____

_____

_____

_____

_____

Purposeful, positive actions I give to others today: _____

_____

_____

_____

_____

_____

_____

What I liked about today/What I didn't like and want to change: _____

_____

_____

_____

_____

_____

Balanced Parenting
✍ My Compass
Day 27

Date:_____

I. My Spiritual Wellness
You will know the truth, and the truth will set you free.
John 8:32, the Bible

Prayer

Contemplating God _____

_____

God, I need to make things right with you with _____

_____

Thank you, God, for _____

_____

God, I need your guidance and help for _____

_____

I ask for wisdom for _____

_____

Reading/Thought for Today

_____

_____

II. My Mental and Emotional Wellness
As a person thinks, so he or she is.
John 8:32, the Bible

Positively Growing My Mind

Reading/audio/video _____

Remember this thought today _____

_____

Beauty appreciated _____

III. My Physical Wellness

Maximum bodily strength and efficiency depend upon three factors:
sleep, exercise, and nutrition.
Dr Martin Shaffer, Life after Stress (New York: Plenum Press, 1982, page 92)

Sleep

Hours:		Quality:					
			Poor	Fair	Moderate	Good	Excellent

Uninterrupted? yes/no _____

Exercise

Aerobic _____

Strength _____

Flexibility _____

Nutrition

Water _____ _____ _____ _____ _____ _____ _____
(check mark per 8 oz.)

Food

Breakfast _____

Snack _____

Lunch _____

Snack _____

Dinner _____

Snack _____

Vitamins/supplements _____

_____

IV. My Social/Relational Wellness

Love is not like other resources.... The more it is used, the more its supply increases.
Dr. Richard Swenson, Margin (Colorado Springs: Navpress, 1992, page 240)

Growing Positive Relationships

Face-to-face with others _____

_____

_____

Phone calls/ written words (email/letters) _____

_____

_____

_____

_____

Purposeful, positive actions I give to others today: _____

_____

_____

_____

_____

_____

_____

What I liked about today/What I didn't like and want to change: _____

_____

_____

_____

_____

_____

Balanced Parenting
✍ My Compass
Day 28

Date:_____

I. My Spiritual Wellness
You will know the truth, and the truth will set you free.
John 8:32, the Bible

Prayer

Contemplating God _____
_____

God, I need to make things right with you with _____
_____

Thank you, God, for _____
_____

God, I need your guidance and help for _____
_____

I ask for wisdom for _____
_____

Reading/Thought for Today

_____
_____

II. My Mental and Emotional Wellness
As a person thinks, so he or she is.
John 8:32, the Bible

Positively Growing My Mind

Reading/audio/video _____

Remember this thought today _____
_____

Beauty appreciated _____

III. My Physical Wellness
Maximum bodily strength and efficiency depend upon three factors:
sleep, exercise, and nutrition.
Dr Martin Shaffer, Life after Stress (New York: Plenum Press, 1982, page 92)

Sleep

Hours:		Quality:					
			Poor	Fair	Moderate	Good	Excellent

Uninterrupted? yes/no _____

Exercise

Aerobic _____

Strength _____

Flexibility _____

Nutrition

Water _____ _____ _____ _____ _____ _____ _____
(check mark per 8 oz.)

Food

Breakfast _____

Snack _____

Lunch _____

Snack _____

Dinner _____

Snack _____

Vitamins/supplements _____

_____

IV. My Social/Relational Wellness

Love is not like other resources.... The more it is used, the more its supply increases.
Dr. Richard Swenson, Margin (Colorado Springs: Navpress, 1992, page 240)

Growing Positive Relationships

Face-to-face with others _____

_____

_____

Phone calls/ written words (email/letters) _____

_____

_____

_____

_____

Purposeful, positive actions I give to others today: _____

_____

_____

_____

_____

_____

_____

What I liked about today/What I didn't like and want to change: _____

_____

_____

_____

_____

_____

Balanced Parenting
✍ My Compass
Day 29

Date:_____

I. My Spiritual Wellness
You will know the truth, and the truth will set you free.
John 8:32, the Bible

Prayer

Contemplating God _____
_____

God, I need to make things right with you with _____
_____

Thank you, God, for _____
_____

God, I need your guidance and help for _____
_____

I ask for wisdom for _____
_____

Reading/Thought for Today

_____
_____

II. My Mental and Emotional Wellness
As a person thinks, so he or she is.
John 8:32, the Bible

Positively Growing My Mind

Reading/audio/video _____

Remember this thought today _____
_____

Beauty appreciated _____

III. My Physical Wellness
Maximum bodily strength and efficiency depend upon three factors:
sleep, exercise, and nutrition.
Dr Martin Shaffer, Life after Stress (New York: Plenum Press, 1982, page 92)

Sleep

Hours:		Quality:	Poor	Fair	Moderate	Good	Excellent

Uninterrupted? yes/no _____

Exercise

Aerobic _____

Strength _____

Flexibility _____

Nutrition

Water _____ _____ _____ _____ _____ _____ _____
(check mark per 8 oz.)

Food

Breakfast _____

Snack _____

Lunch _____

Snack _____

Dinner _____

Snack _____

Vitamins/supplements _____

_____

IV. My Social/Relational Wellness

Love is not like other resources.... The more it is used, the more its supply increases.
Dr. Richard Swenson, Margin (Colorado Springs: Navpress, 1992, page 240)

Growing Positive Relationships

Face-to-face with others _____

_____

_____

Phone calls/ written words (email/letters) _____

_____

_____

_____

_____

Purposeful, positive actions I give to others today: _____

_____

_____

_____

_____

_____

_____

What I liked about today/What I didn't like and want to change: _____

_____

_____

_____

_____

_____

Balanced Parenting
✍ My Compass
Day 30

Date:_____

I. My Spiritual Wellness
You will know the truth, and the truth will set you free.
John 8:32, the Bible

Prayer

Contemplating God _____

_____

God, I need to make things right with you with _____

_____

Thank you, God, for _____

_____

God, I need your guidance and help for _____

_____

I ask for wisdom for _____

_____

Reading/Thought for Today

_____

_____

II. My Mental and Emotional Wellness
As a person thinks, so he or she is.
John 8:32, the Bible

Positively Growing My Mind

Reading/audio/video _____

Remember this thought today _____

_____

Beauty appreciated _____

III. My Physical Wellness
Maximum bodily strength and efficiency depend upon three factors:
sleep, exercise, and nutrition.
Dr Martin Shaffer, Life after Stress (New York: Plenum Press, 1982, page 92)

Sleep

Hours:		Quality:		Poor	Fair	Moderate	Good	Excellent

Uninterrupted? yes/no _____

Exercise

Aerobic _____

Strength _____

Flexibility _____

Nutrition

Water _____ _____ _____ _____ _____ _____ _____
(check mark per 8 oz.)

Food

Breakfast _____

Snack _____

Lunch _____

Snack _____

Dinner _____

Snack _____

Vitamins/supplements _____

_____

IV. My Social/Relational Wellness

Love is not like other resources.... The more it is used, the more its supply increases.
Dr. Richard Swenson, Margin (Colorado Springs: Navpress, 1992, page 240)

Growing Positive Relationships

Face-to-face with others _____

_____

_____

Phone calls/ written words (email/letters) _____

_____

_____

_____

_____

Purposeful, positive actions I give to others today: _____

_____

_____

_____

_____

_____

_____

What I liked about today/What I didn't like and want to change: _____

_____

_____

_____

_____

_____

When your 30 Days of Journaling are Complete

You've made changes, felt the winds of momentum toward your goals, and experienced new achievements resulting in a lifestyle bringing lifelong change. Bravo for creating changes you and your relationship to your child for the better – *forever!*

The result of working through a program like this is that you develop patterns of behavior – ways to "think and do" – that become more deeply embedded into who you are. The more you go through this program, the more healthy thoughts and behaviors are embedded into who you are and how you act – and the more you *live and thrive.*

Like in the game, "Mother May I," our life moves forward in steps: Sometimes they're giant steps, sometimes they're baby steps. Each time you return to use this workbook, you take giant steps. The most important thing is to keep moving forward, no matter *what* the size of the steps.

The Teeter Totter

Remember, this workbook helps the teeter totter of your life return to balance. Expect the teeter totter to tip again – because it absolutely will! That is the nature of our lives as moms and dads. And that is the nature of being human. Plan for it! Then, when it does tip to the side, *don't panic.* Don't get discouraged. Don't throw up your hands and give up. Just do something about it. Return to this workbook. Go through this guidebook again and again. You'll find yourself returning to balance, no matter how busy life gets.

Part Six

Your Child

୬ଡ଼ଌ

Finding Balance with Your Child

Creating and Balancing Time
With Your Son or Daughter

୬ଡ଼ଌ

Our most precious gift is our child.
If we take time to learn how to think clearly and in healthy ways,
feel strongly in commitment and sensitivity,
and act wisely in our every day responses,
then we'll fully enjoy that precious gift
as he or she was meant to be enjoyed.
~EBC

Healthy parents raise healthy children. Now that we're finding balance in our own lives, we can find balance in loving and responding to our child.

This section is a 40 day "bonus" to take your relationship to your child to new heights. You're balancing your busy life; now grow deeper in your relationship with your child.

▶ What's this About?

If we desire balance with our child, then we must be fully aware of how we're spending time with and impacting our child on a daily basis. We must choose to spend our time in a way that impacts our child with love and purposeful creation of relationship. Only then will we feel satisfied that we're giving our child all we can give. Only then will we know that we're being the best parent that we can be. Only then will we spend our time with our child with meaningful actions – in a way that truly builds a relationship with our child that lasts.

✓ To Do

Use the following journal the same way that you used your personal journal. There's only one page here, though; photocopy however many pages you'd like. I encourage you to set aside at least another 40 days to become aware of your child's spiritual, mental, physical, and social life. Purposefully create the relationship you want with your child. Your relationship will deepen into more interaction, more connection, and more joy in the next 40 days.

Here's an example page:

Balanced Parenting ♥ Loving My Child

Day/Date: _____*Friday, June 24*_____

I. My Child's Spiritual Wellness

Prayer

Thank you, God, for my child's *happy spirit he wakes up with__*
*_____ energy and joy - smiling and excited to talk_*

God, I need your guidance and help for *how best to help him to get*
__along with his brother - they seem to always be picking on each other!

I ask for wisdom for ____ *the right time to encourage and the right time to*
_____discipline; his "energy" keeps getting him in trouble!!!_

Thought for Today

God, I know you care about the relationship with me and my son. If I just turn to
you and talk to you about it, I'm sure You'll give me help. I can do this!

II. My Child's Mental and Emotional Wellness

Positively Growing My Child's Mind

Reading/audio/video *Read a story about self control together at*
_____ bedtime _____

Purposefully teach this thought today *We all have choices to make*
_____he can decide to make good choices__

Beauty appreciated together *_____Missed this today - felt too busy*
And rushed between school and home, dinner, etc.!
CHANGE THIS TOMORROW!

III. My Child's Physical Wellness

Sleep

Hours:	~ 9 ½	Quality:		X			
(9ish to 6:45 AM)			Poor	Fair	Moderate	Good	Excellent

Uninterrupted? *No* -- *had a bad dream around 1AM*

Exercise

I'm not sure about this....playground at school?
(ASK TOMORROW ABOUT THIS)

Nutrition

Water *sent water bottle to school; think he used it – check backpack*

Food

Breakfast *bowl of corn flake cereal and milk_*

Snack *wheat crackers and peanut butter, cup of milk*

Lunch *turkey sandwich, carrot sticks, brownie, cup of milk*

Snack *apple slices, milk*
        (think he might have snuck something out of the cupboard, too...)

Dinner *mac & cheese (added "real" cheese"), didn't eat green beans, milk, orange*
        slice

Snack *finished two orange slices left from dinner time*

Vitamins/Supplements *daily vitamin in AM, gave Omegas at dinner*

IV. Social/Relational Wellness

Growing Positive Relationships

Purposeful relationship time with my child _____ *read one book at bedtime only...again – felt soooo rushed today!*

My child's time with others *neighbor came over for a half hour*

Purposeful, positive actions my child and I give to others together today

Called Grandma after dinner – talked about 15 minutes. Felt good about this. Put another call in calendar for next week.

_____

_____

_____

Now it's your turn. Copy the next pages and purposefully craft your relationship with your child...

Balanced Parenting ♥ Loving My Child

Day/Date: _____

I. My Child's Spiritual Wellness

Prayer

Thank you, God, for my child's _____
_____

God, I need your guidance and help for _____
_____

I ask for wisdom for _____
_____

Thought for Today

_____
_____

II. My Child's Mental and Emotional Wellness

Positively Growing My Child's Mind

Reading/audio/video _____
_____

Purposefully teach this thought today _____
_____

Beauty appreciated together _____
_____

III. My Child's Physical Wellness

Sleep

Hours:		Quality:					
			Poor	Fair	Moderate	Good	Excellent

Uninterrupted? _____

Exercise

_____

_____

Nutrition

Water _____

Food

Breakfast _____

Snack _____

Lunch _____

Snack _____

_____

Dinner _____

_____

Snack _____

_____

Vitamins/Supplements _____

_____

IV. Social/Relational Wellness

Growing Positive Relationships

Purposeful relationship time with my child _____

_____

My child's time with others _____

_____

Purposeful, positive actions my child and I give to others together today

_____

_____

_____

_____

_____

About the Author
Erin Brown Conroy, MA, MFA

Personal Information

Erin has 13 children by birth, marriage, and adoption and lives in Southwest Michigan, where she writes, teaches, speaks, and home schools her youngest two children who are still living at home.

Authorship/Books/Magazines

In addition to the books listed below, Erin has authored numerous articles and educational materials, including over 40 complete online courses for children and adults and entire online writing programs. Erin has been quoted in hundreds of online articles (including *iparenting.com, familyresource.com, geoparent.com*), newspapers (including *The Chicago Tribune, Dallas Morning News,* and the *Miami Herald*), and parenting magazines (including Parents magazine and Parenting magazine). She was a parenting columnist for Great Lakes Family Magazine (4 years) and Jen Singer's MommaSaid.net web site for stay-at-home moms (6 years).

Speaking/Radio

For over 30 years (since the 1980's), Erin has been a speaker at educational conferences and conventions, for national organizations (such as McDonald's), for homeschooling groups and conferences. Since 2004, Erin has been a guest on radio shows for parenting and child development including WGN Chicago (three-time guest to *The Steve Cochran Show*), *Parent Talk Radio, Family Matters Radio, The Doctor Laura Berman Show,* and *Real Life with Darla Shine.*

Education

Erin has a Bachelor's degree in education (1981, Western Michigan University) and a Master's degree in a rehabilitation field (1991, Western Michigan University) with special education and physical impairment emphasis. She completed a terminal degree (MFA) in 2015 at Western State Colorado University in Writing, with a Genre Fiction emphasis.

University and Online Teaching

From 2001 to 2008, and then again 2015 to the present, Erin has been an adjunct professor with Cornerstone University's Professional and Graduate Studies Division (Grand Rapids, Michigan; Kalamazoo and St. Joseph sites) in leadership, management, professional development, personal communication skills, college success skills, writing, research, and health and wellness.

From 2007 to 2013, Erin was the distance learning writing instructor for Patrick Henry College (Purcellville, VA), teaching College-Level Writing Skills and Research and Writing. She developed and taught the courses on line, coached college student in fiction writing, and presented seminars to the student body on writing effectively.

Erin designed and, since 2009, has been the Master Teacher for HSLDA Academy (formerly Patrick Henry College Preparatory Academy) for the AP English Language and Composition course, where she presently oversees the Lead Teacher and Classroom Teachers. Erin also designed the HomeschoolConnections.com Aquinas Writing Advantage program for middle and high school students online, where she has been the Master Teacher/Coordinator (since 2011) for the program's staff of classroom instructors and grading services instructors.

Teaching Reading

Erin developed, taught, and tested the *True North Reading, The Complete Mastery Reading & Spelling Program* for the past 20+ years—a five-level multisensory learn-to-read program for children ages 2 to 15 that is found at www.truenorthreading.com. She speaks across the nation on teaching and learning, reading, and writing (since the mid 1980s) and has consulted privately both in person and remotely regarding reading, spelling, writing, and test preparation for over 30 years.

Professional Memberships

Erin is a member of the Society of Children's Book Writers and Illustrators (SCBWA), the American Christian Fiction Writer's Association (ACFW), and Science Fiction and Fantasy Writers of America (SWFA).

Latest Publications

The book, *Simplified Writing 101: Top Secrets for College Success*, was released in 2013. Five additional writing books are planned, along with *The Master 7 Principle*, which outlines the seven skills needed to learn anything successfully.

Just for fun...

When not teaching or speaking, Erin loves playing the wooden flute and hanging out with her teens and three dogs.

Visit Erin's blog for creatives, writers, and entrepreneurs at *erinbrownconroy.wordpress.com*.

Get Erin's books on *www.amazon.com*.

Get information and help your child learn to read at *www.TrueNorthReading.com*.